SMACKS AND BAWLEYS

by

JOHN LEATHER

TERENCE DALTON LIMITED
LAVENHAM   SUFFOLK
1991

Published by
TERENCE DALTON LIMITED

ISBN 0 86138 079 7

Text photoset in 10/12 pt Baskerville

Printed in Great Britain at
The Lavenham Press Limited, Lavenham, Suffolk

Contents

Index of Illustrations

INTRODUCTION

SEVERAL books exist which in part tell of the sailing fishing smacks and bawleys of the coast of Essex and the north coast of Kent. This is the first book devoted to an overview of the subject, bringing together a representative selection of photographs and prints of the craft and their crews from the many small ports where they were owned, built and manned. Many of these villages and small towns now have little significance or connection with fishing, yet in their day, which in many instances extended over many generations and several centuries, these were strongholds of good fishermen and seamen, who used good stout vessels and also supported thriving industries ashore, from shipwrights and sailmakers to oyster merchants and sprat curers.

The development of the Essex and the Whitstable and Medway oyster fisheries extended over several centuries. The great Essex fishery for sprats and the slightly lesser ones for bottom fish and shrimps were supplemented by many other minor fishing activities, some of which are still carried on under power. These fisheries resulted in the evolution of the cutter-rigged sailing smack in a form suited to these fisheries and its bringing to near perfection for its purpose within the available and affordable technology. In contrast to the larger smacks, with their elegant counters, the Thames and Medway peter boat also evolved into a transom-sterned cutter and eventually into the larger bawley.

Development was slow but continuous until the early nineteenth century, but by its middle years these craft were enjoying their final and most advanced form, arrangements and rig. The fleets reached a peak in the 1880s but started to decline in numbers by the turn of the century. A century ago many hundreds of smacks and bawleys were in use, making their white sails as ubiquitous in the Essex or Kentish seascape as the tan ones of the sailing barges and the stout canvas of other small cargo-carrying fore and aft and square-rigged vessels that made up the bulk of local merchant shipping. As with certain other periods of history, a war (1914–18) was a watershed in the Essex and Kent fisheries. After it the decline accelerated, despite the adoption of engines; at first as auxiliary power, then, by the nineteen-thirties, as the prime mover. Sailing smacks and a very few sailing bawleys lingered into the nineteen-thirties, and in the oyster fisheries of the Blackwater and at Whitstable into the nineteen-forties, with the little Maldon smacks being perhaps the very last to work under sail in the nineteen-fifties, though they then also had auxiliary engines.

By the nineteen-sixties sailing smacks and bawleys, their fishing gear and way of life, had passed into history. However, the interest and efforts of some enthusiasts, before the present cult of restoring gaff-rigged and other old craft had taken hold in the early nineteen-sixties, resulted in several smaller smacks being carefully restored and rebuilt to be privately maintained in a sailing and fishing condition. An annual focus for this splendid private effort was the West Mersea Town Regatta smack race, which was revived in 1947 after several years' lapse and remains the doyen of the many similar events now held on this coast.

By about 1962 the sailing, restoration and even building of gaff-rigged craft gathered momentum, perhaps as a reaction against the advanced technology of the modern sailing yacht. The smacks and bawleys of Essex and Kent were amongst the larger craft benefiting from this enthusiasm and this has continued, until a quarter century later one may now sail in a smack of some 50 feet, or a bawley, up to about 38 feet and experience the joys, terrors and trials of craft which were new perhaps a century ago and in which the ancestors of some of us found their living.

In the wake of this revival other smaller craft of the area have been sought out and restored. In at least one instance, the splendid Gravesend shrimper *Marigold* has been rebuilt. It is now possible to examine, and perhaps to sail in, other local types, such as cocklers, peter boats, dobles and bumkins. This picturesque name was the fisherman's term for small open dredging and trawling boats which were sailed like the winklers' craft and some sailing oyster and trawling skiffs. Records have also been made of other types such as sprat punts and smack's boats. The origin of the name of the peter boat, this craft so peculiar to the Thames, is obscure, but some historians have sought to link it with St Peter. The keys of St Peter, patron saint of fishermen, form part of the armorial bearings of the Fishmongers' Company of London. It is possible that the peter boat first received its name when Mellitus, who was consecrated Bishop of the East Saxons at London by Augustine of Canterbury in the seventh century, founded a cathedral church dedicated to St Peter on the island of Thorney. Perhaps it was thought to be similar in shape to the fishing boat used by Peter on the Sea of Gallilee. This is an engaging thought but purely conjectural, and the truth is that we cannot be certain of when or how the peter boat came by its name.

My grandfather, James Barnard, my great-grandfather, Thomas Barnard and his father were all owners of smacks from the Essex village of Rowhedge, as were their many brothers, as also were my grandmother's brothers and father, the Cranfields. They owned many craft, ranging from the 45–50 foot eighteen tonners, common at the end of the nineteenth century and into the early twentieth, to the 65 foot and 70 foot cutters and ketches of the mid-Victorian heyday; the bold salvagers, deep-sea oyster dredgers, scallopers, occasional smugglers and pilot boats—the first class smacks of local legend.

In writing this book I feel that in a way I have repaid a debt to the memory of these fine seamen and fishermen whose skill, enterprise and achievements were in danger of being forgotten by the nineteen-forties and -fifties, when most of their contemporaries, captains and crews, were passing on. As a descendant of some of them I have tried for more than forty years to record as much as possible and complement this with extensive research. The wider aspects of their story are given in my earlier books, *The Northseamen* and *The Salty Shore*, while *Saltwater Village*, written by my mother, Margaret Leather, vividly recalls her childhood and early life as Margaret Barnard, daughter of a smack owner and yacht skipper in the Rowhedge of the early years of this century. It is a valuable piece of social history.

Although the sailing smacks and the fishing gear they used now look antiquated, these were generally efficient in the context of their times and costs. Over many generations the enterprise of the men who sailed them ensured the survival of their communities. They served not only as fishermen but aboard yachts and in the merchant service.

With the exception of the Colne and Blackwater men's yacht-racing exploits, which were their great pride, these seafarers thought their way of life unremarkable and certainly did not consider themselves privileged to experience it, for it was often harsh for them and their families. What they longed for most was security of employment, which very few achieved. Ownership of their own smack and their own house was the aim of most. For their sons they wished the best career they could achieve, at sea or elsewhere.

This book is written as a contribution to the record of a now vanished style of seafaring carried on by men who deserve to be remembered.

John Leather

X

CHAPTER ONE

Greenwich to Gravesend

UNTIL the mid-nineteenth century the tidal Thames supported a lively and mixed fishing activity. Many foreshores, from Rotherhithe downstream to Leigh on the Essex shore and Gravesend on the Kent side, were the homes of fishermen finding a poor living with distinct but humble craft. They worked craft from little 12 foot peter boats to bold bawleys up to about 38 foot length, trawling for shrimps, bottom fish and eels; seining for mullet and smelts, occasionally dredging for oysters and at times setting long lines for bottom fish. The fisheries of the tideway survived reasonably well until the mid-nineteenth century, when industrial and domestic pollution and a great increase in shipping, particularly steamships, began to ruin the salt-water Thames.

The peter boat had the oldest associations with the river. It was originally a pointed-stern, clench-built, rowed fishing boat with a wet well amidships to keep the catch alive until it was landed. It was developed to set a sprit mainsail and a staysail, but had no bowsprit. There are references to craft of this type at "Lye" (Leigh, Essex) in 1540. The smaller sizes were used as far upstream as Chiswick and the larger ones fished from Barking, Leigh and other estuary ports, with some fishing coastwise to the rivers Crouch and Roach, Blackwater and Colne and sometimes to the Suffolk Stour and Orwell. Others sometimes fished the Kentish shore as far east as Margate.

In its basic form the peter boat was a 12–14 foot, pointed-stern boat of good depth. It could be rowed easily, and if necessary when fishing it could be rowed stern first. The usual crew was two men. There were side decks set about four inches below the sheerstrake, which had no gunwale so that nets and headropes slid over unhindered when setting nets. Large numbers of these boats were in use and typical dimensions were 14 foot length by 5 foot beam by 2 foot depth.

The peter net was a small seine, about 20 to 25 fathoms in length, but it did not have a pocket to collect the catch. It was set in various ways by fishermen from different places in the area. Small peter boats used it principally as a seine to be set around a shoal of fish, leaving a buoy at one end which would be retrieved when encirclement was completed and the ends of the net hauled together. Besides surrounding shoals of fish, peter nets were much used for stopping creeks, set across the waterways with stakes to support them at low water and left until the next ebb, when the fishermen came downstream flailing oars on the surface to frighten fish into the nets. Stop-netting was made illegal but that did not stop the peter boat men. Many peter boats laid in the Thames tideway with a small conical-shaped stowboat net lowered over the bow in a miniature of the large nets worked by the Essex smacks. Small peter boats of about 14–16 foot length were used under oars in some Essex rivers, in the same manner as those on the Thames, and were of the same construction and arrangement.

Peter boats had considerable rise of floor, and although fairly fine at the waterline endings they were full in the bow and stern above water. The stem profile was rounded and the sternpost slightly less so, but with a rake. The rockered keel protruded only slightly below the garboard strakes to assist the boat when turning under oars, which was also why the hull was kept as small as possible, consistent with seaworthiness and range of use. The clinker planking was laid on sawn oak frames, notched over the lands. There were short forward and after decks set four inches to six inches below the top of the sheerstrake and drained through it by small scupper holes. A coaming of about that height was set across from sheer to sheer at the forward end of the cockpit, and side deck coamings were carried to the after coaming, which might be square across the boat or was sometimes rounded. In small peter boats the rower sat on the enclosed, watertight, wooden well, which was connected to the water by small holes through the hull planking. Fish were put into this through a small hatch in its top and while the boat floated were kept alive until they were landed. Peter boats were among the earliest wet-well fishing boats in western countries, though wells were used earlier in China and possibly elsewhere.

The oars were of heavy, rectangular section inboard of the rowlocks to assist balance and allow the rower to let go of them suddenly when fishing without their slipping out of the wooden rowlocks on the sheerstrakes.

Peter boats of all sizes were rigged for sailing, the smallest with a boomless spritsail lashed at the throat to an unstayed mast and a foresail hanked to the forestay or set flying, tacked to the stemhead. Peter boats had no centreboards and relied on the fine ends to work to windward. The spritsails of the larger boats had a single brail from the throat to the leech, and larger sprits might have a yard tackle to set them up and support them.

Some larger, open sailing peter boats rigged a canvas tilt for shelter at anchor over half round hoops, with the mast and sprit lowered and lashed down from the forward and after decks on the centreline. This allowed the crew to work away from home for a few days, and little groups of tilted peter boats gathered in the lee of Thames foreshores for shelter overnight or during bad weather, smoke drifting from a stovepipe poked through the tilt. These sailing peter boats used below London might have been 19 foot by 7 foot by 3 foot depth.

Larger peter boats existed by the end of the eighteenth century: the 25 foot 3 inches *Friends Goodwill* was launched in 1790 and the 26 foot *Good Intent* was built in 1797 with a "round" (pointed) stern, suggesting that transom-sterned examples were then known.

When peter boats became too large to be easily manoeuvred under oars to work a net the usefulness of the pointed stern was gone and the less expensive transom stern began to be used, as it increased working space aft and improved stability under sail. Size also increased for some fisheries, particularly shrimping and whitebait stow-netting. Some set a sprit or lug mizzen and many had a portable wooden cabin-top over the space between the foredeck and the wet well.

Latter-day transom-sterned peter boats ranged up to about 30 feet in length and worked to most parts of the Thames and its estuary. Peter boats from Barking Creek and Gravesend were regularly fishing at West Mersea during the eighteen-seventies, but by then the type had become transom-sterned gaff cutters and their crews visited the Blackwater in season to stop-net the creeks for flounders.

Many peter boats were also owned at Leigh, the ancient fishing village on a creek to the west of the modern pleasure resort of Southend on Sea, then an isolated rural village. Here, as elsewhere in many places on the lower Thames, the larger peter boats retained the spritsail rig until the mid-nineteenth century and became known as pinks, from the pointed stern. The pink seems to have been a transitional type from the small peter boat to the gaff-rigged bawley. Those at Leigh were usually decked and set a sprit mainsail with a topsail over carried on a topmast, a staysail, and a jib set on a bowsprit of modest length. They did not have a windlass for the anchor cable.

These boats worked mainly between the Nore Sand and Holehaven, at the upper end of Sea Reach, at Canvey Island. Most had a wet well amidships which was carried the full breadth of the hull up to around the waterline then rose in a tapering trunk to reduce the free surface effect of the water in it from adversely affecting stability.

About 1830 the *King William IV* was launched as the first Leigh peter boat with a transom stern. Only half a dozen were built during the next ten years, but gradually the pinks and peter boats at Leigh were replaced by this transom-sterned version, which developed into the powerful, gaff rigged and carvel-planked bawleys described in chapter four.

Besides the smaller pointed-stern type larger transom-sterned peter boats were also built and owned as far up the salt-water Thames as Greenwich. The larger Greenwich boats were about 24–26 feet long by the 1830s and carried the boomless gaff mainsail, topsail, staysail and jib of the later Leigh or Harwich bawleys, though the hulls remained clinker planked. Many had wet wells and most fished for whitebait in season with a stow net of a size suited to their dimensions. They worked in the various reaches of the river below Greenwich and perhaps even down to Sea Reach, some distance from their home port. However, river pollution increased by the later nineteenth century and many owners moved downstream, some to Leigh in Essex and perhaps others to Erith or Gravesend on the Kent shore.

Amongst these emigrants were the Young family from Greenwich, who had for many years worked the 27 foot peter boat *Favourite* in the whitebait fishery, for which her unusually deep draught of 6 feet may have been an advantage in keeping her steady while lying to the net. They also owned a similar peter boat, but towards the end of the century pollution in the upper reaches drove them down to settle at Leigh, where they continued the whitebait trade until the nineteen-sixties.

Erith was then a small community of barge-owning and fishing families. Both barges and fishing vessels were built there by the yard of Douglas Stone, an enterprising designer and an excellent practical shipwright and boatbuilder, who had served his apprenticeship at John Harvey's shipyard at Wivenhoe. He constructed several good sailing bawleys and is credited as being the first to install a wheel in a spritsail barge, the *Anglo Norman* in 1882. Several notably fast barges were built by Stone, and his bawleys had a high reputation. The lines and sail plan of the 32 foot *May Flower* LO 180 are shown in fig 6 as typical of his work. The *May Flower* was designed to be as fast as possible consistent with hold capacity and the light draught required by her owner. She had the reputation, when new in the eighteen-eighties of being the fastest bawley in the lower Thames. Stone gave her a little more freeboard than usual to keep her decks drier in the short steep seas of the Lower Hope and Sea Reach, where the Erith and Gravesend boats then principally fished.

By then almost all bawleys were being built with carvel planking and with a "dry bottom" in which a wet well was not fitted. We may be sure that the bawleys Stone launched were well finished, as he also built and designed small yachts. In the 1890s he moved to the Essex port of Brightlingsea, where he continued to design and build yachts of many rigs and types, some barges and a few sailing smacks and bawleys. The business survived in modern form as the steel shipyard of James and Stone Ltd, which sadly closed in 1988.

Besides the peter boats and bawleys the rough, tidal waters of the lower Thames developed another type of pointed-sterned, clinker-planked, beamy and decked spritsail-rigged fishing craft known as a "hatch boat". This name derived, perhaps, from the long, narrow cockpit ending in a small forward cabin top over the accommodation. Hatch boats were often 30 feet long and had a wet well like the peter boats, whose rig of spritsail and foresail they at first carried. Later a topmast and topsail were set above a sprit mainsail and a jib set on a running bowsprit. The mainsheet worked on a horse above the tiller and the mainsail had a single brail to the throat. Many of the largest stepped a spritsail mizzen with the boom sheeting to the top of the sternpost, a rig of yawl proportions. These boats were steered with a rudder head yoke and tiller lines. Many were fast and the lines appear well formed and fine in all contemporary prints, (fig. 4).

The hatch boat seems to have evolved from the Thames wherry rather than the peter boat. The wherries were a type of Thames rowing boat for passenger carrying. Hatch boats had the wherry's buoyant bow and flared sides above the waterline. By the early nineteenth century many hatch boats had adopted the standing gaff mainsail with the gaff controlled by vangs to the peak, though a sprit mizzen was retained. Hatch boats fished the Kent and Essex shores from the North Foreland to the river Blackwater, usually with peter nets and dredges. A few migrated to fish out of Maldon and possibly West Mersea, in Essex. As many as 635 hatch boats were sailing in 1854, making them the most prolific Thames fishing craft of any size, but only ninety-seven were recorded in 1863. By this time the cutter-rigged smacks and bawleys, more suited to trawling for the quickly growing city markets, were multiplying fast.

Many hatch boats were owned at Gravesend, the once busy pilot town on the Kent shore of the lower Thames which was the anchorage for vessels entering or leaving the London river. In later years a score or so of small bawleys and the similar, local style shrimpers worked from there, lying at moorings off the town in what came to be known as Bawley Bay. These craft continued to find a living under sail into the nineteen-twenties, but despite the installation of engines numbers declined rapidly during the nineteen-thirties and by 1960 only two or three Gravesend craft remained, trawling under power in a sadly polluted river. One of the last, the *Ellen*, was worked by James Bradford and William Warner, one of a Gravesend family whose fishing activities extended back into the eighteenth century.

The *Ellen* was reputedly built at Gravesend about 1780. She was 28 feet 6 inches long and her hull was clinker planked, making her akin to, if not one of, the transom, sterned peter boats. Originally she had a fish well in the bottom arranged as has already been described. Other similar shrimpers built and owned at Gravesend were the *Fiddle*, *Charlotte* and *Lillian*, which were about 30 feet long with 11 foot beam and 3 foot 6 inches draught. The smaller *Saucy Lass*, *Three Sisters* and others were about 25 feet long by 9 foot 6 inches beam and 2 foot 9 inches draught. There were also other small bawleys which had been sold to Gravesend owners from Leigh when rapid increase in the size of Leigh boats took place after the middle of the nineteenth century. The small size of these fishing boats was suited to their work, which was mainly in the Lower Hope and Sea Reach.

Old ways seemed to survive longest at Gravesend, where the shrimpers used a variation of the beam net that was in use at Leigh until the end of the nineteenth century. In essentials this was a form of beam trawl, but instead of a ground rope a lower beam of oak was used. This was about 9 feet long and had about 25 pounds of lead run into recesses on its upper face as ballast. It was shod with iron on the underside where it dragged along the bottom. A short strut about 18 inches long was fixed upright in a chock at the centre of its top. This supported a parallel upper beam about 6 feet long. A three-span bridle from the lower beam and the top beam led to the warp. The net was about 12 feet long with a space left between its forward bottom edge and the lower beam to reduce the stones and rubbish gathered. Two or more of these nets could be worked by a shrimper. They were hauled individually.

Until the nineteen-fifties the Gravesend shrimpers used the "trim tram", as the Leigh fishermen had until they adopted the beam trawl for shrimping in the later nineteenth century. This gear also had a horizontal ground beam, from the middle of which two horizontal wooden arms formed a triangle with an iron-shod apex which acted as stabilising ballast and allowed it to travel over the ground like a sledge, without digging in. The net could be made from a rectangle folded to shape. Its mouth was also held open by a strut and upper beam. This ancient form of trawl was worked by some of the last shrimpers to belong to Gravesend in the nineteen-sixties, of which the *Ellen* was probably the last. This old gear remained in use because of the smooth ground, the confined and traffic-ridden waters worked by the Gravesend boats and also because such nets could if necessary be quickly hauled and shot again.

In winter some Gravesend bawleys and a few of the shrimpers went stowboating for sprats in the lower Thames, when shrimps were scarce. However, the boats really lacked the capacity for this work and were too small to ride anchored with a heavy net. The *Ellen* could carry only 200 bushels and the *Charlotte* about 160, offering at best a poor return for outlay in nets and labour.

Some larger bawleys based at Gravesend at the end of the nineteenth century and early in the twentieth century were used as boarding tenders for pilots, serving ships entering or leaving the London river in and around the Lower Hope, Sea Reach and the estuary. These carried the usual bawley rig and when on service flew a large pilot flag at the topmast head. Other similar craft were used as wreck-marking bawleys by the PLA, often having to anchor near a sunken vessel in the lower reaches to warn off other shipping. For this purpose these bawleys had the word *WRECK* painted along their bulwarks amidships and flew a warning signal. At night two lanterns were shown from the arms of the crosstrees. These bawleys were still in use during the nineteen-twenties, but seem to have died out soon after.

A score of shrimping bawleys and the smaller shrimpers fished from Gravesend in the nineteen-thirties, but numbers had declined by 1948, when there were sixteen left and one larger smack, the *Freda*, lying in Bawley Bay on the foreshore. During 1945 brown shrimps were trawled in marketable quantities on the north shore of the Thames near Gravesend, but increasing pollution forced the boats to seek shrimps as far downstream as Southend by the nineteen-fifties. I recall seeing the little fleet of Gravesend vessels working about the Blyth Sand at that time while I was spending holidays in the Leigh motor shrimper *Boy David* with Arthur Cotgrove. *Providence, Daisy, Amy, Lillian, Fiddle* and *Eleanor* were working full time and the *Thistle* part time. The last purely sailing bawleys from Gravesend were the *May Queen* and the *Seven Brothers*, both of which finished shrimping before 1939.

One of the last to fish from Gravesend was the little *Ellen*, which worked under motor until 1961. In that year, when her owner retired, she was sold to become a tender. The *Thistle* remained at Gravesend a little longer, still with sails bent. Ted Burburry's bawley *Clive Miriam* was the last full-time Gravesend shrimper, and other old bawleys and shrimpers there were being sold as uneconomic craft. Some were bought to be restored for pleasure sailing and fishing, and the little *Lilian* LO 158, particularly, succeeded in perpetuating the type.

The hull lines were taken from the *Lilian* by her new owner, Mr David Patience, who, with the assistance of two boatbuilders, built a replica of her, named *Marigold*, at the premises of Walter Cook and Son Ltd at Maldon, Essex. The hull form of this little vessel is surprisingly fine. The sections have considerable rise of floor and a slack bilge. The entrance is fine and the run long and fair. Such a hull needs legs to take hard ground safely and these were used by bawleys at Gravesend.

I saw the clinker-planked hull of the new shrimper several times during her construction and when fully planked I thought she would be tender under sail. The rig was reconstructed as a close approximation of the original, which had long been discarded. The mast in these shrimpers is stepped exceptionally far forward, probably resulting from their peter boat origins. In the peter boat the sheeting arrangement of the sprit mainsail determines that the mast is stepped further forward than it would be for a boomed sail. The *Marigold's* mainsail is, of course, boomless and has a long gaff. A small foresail sets to the stemhead and the usual bawley-style topsail is carried. Several sizes of jib may be set on the long bowsprit.

The deck arrangements include the long, narrow steering well aft of the shrimper and a small coach roof over the forward accommodation. The mast steps through this against a heavy deck beam. A wooden barrel windlass and the staysail and mainsheet horses complete the arrangements on deck, which is surrounded by a low bulwark.

The original *Lilian* had a wet well built into her bottom amidships with its trunk carried to the deck, but this was of course not needed in the new boat. Gravesend shrimpers had an anchor-cable davit to carry the chain clear of the stem, an unusual feature also seen in some large peter boats.

With many others I awaited the appearance of the *Marigold* with great interest, questioning particularly her ability to carry sail. I first saw her entering the River Colne, standing well up in a fresh breeze and moving fast. The *Marigold* looks certain to carry the form, rig and arrangements of the old large peter boats into the twenty-first century.

7

Fig. 1.   A Thames peter boat of the original, pointed-stern type. The rower sits on the fish well, pulling oars with rectangular looms working in wooden crutches. His mate hauls a peter net, a form of seine net, over the stern. Hundreds of these handy little craft, in size from about 12 feet to around 20 feet or so, fished the river Thames from Teddington downstream, or even above it, to Gravesend and Leigh in the lower reaches. In the Medway a variant was known as a doble.

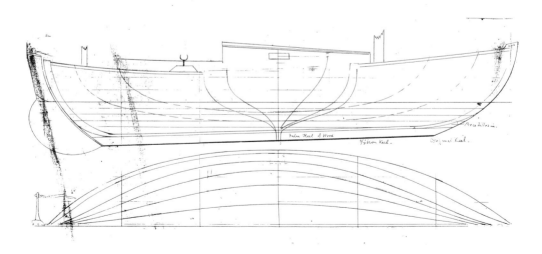

Fig. 3. Thames peter boats. The longer boat, about 18 feet, shows the well-curved stem and sternpost and the usual three rowing ports cut into the sheerstrake. Peter boats were frequently rowed, and most of their work with nets and lines was under oars as the pointed-stern hull could be propelled forward or astern without need to turn. The smaller peter boat in the foreground, perhaps 14 feet long, shows the wet well built into the hull amidships to keep fish fresh for market. The iron horses forward and aft of the cockpit are for the foresail and sprit mainsail sheets. The peter boat in the river, beyond, shows the appearance with the mainsail brailed to the mast and the foresail stowed. The deck was sunk slightly below the sheer. The planking of these boats was usually well lined out and was often of oak on sawn-oak frames. Most lasted for many years despite almost daily use in the river fisheries.

Opposite page, bottom: Fig. 2. Lines of a Gravesend peter boat built about 1835 and later owned by yacht designer and artist Albert Strange, who made this drawing as she was in 1891. The original keel, stem and stern profiles can be seen, a false keel, deck, cabin top, cockpit and mizzen mast having been added for use as a yacht. The sprit mainsail of 75 square feet and foresail of 26 square feet were the original sails. The well-formed hull sections with easy waterlines and buttocks emphasise that a peter boat was rowed as much as sailed, particularly in contrary winds and when working fishing gear. The original shallow keel assisted turning the boat under oars, and a centreplate or daggerboard were not fitted in any, as far as is known. Peter boats sailed well on a close fetch, a reach or run but were slow in turning to windward.

This is the only known scale lines plan of a Thames peter boat. All peter boats are thought to have been built to two or three simple moulds set up on the keel, and in some instances reputedly without moulds of any kind, with the sides differing slightly in form as a result.

9

Fig. 4. A Thames hatch boat. These clinker-planked, beamy fishing boats were rigged with a sprit mainsail, which suggests they developed as a larger version of the peter boat. In later years a boomless gaff mainsail was adopted by many, linking them to the transom-sterned larger peter boats and the later bawley. The rig of the hatch boats finally comprised, besides the mainsail, a foresail, jib set on a bowsprit, a topsail and a mizzen which might be a spritsail or a lug. The average length was 30 feet and many were fast boats. Steering was with a rudder head yoke and tiller lines.
The hatch boats were used for fishing with peter nets, lines, dredges and light trawls. The type was to be found from London downstream to the North Foreland in Kent and northward to the river Blackwater in Essex. They were a prolific type: 635 were recorded in use in 1854.

Top right: Fig. 5. The hull of the new Gravesend shrimper *Marigold*, completed in the shed of Walter Cook and Son Ltd at Maldon, Essex, in 1978. This beautifully-built replica of a Gravesend sailing bawley or large peter boat was given a reconstructed rig setting a generous sail area. She sails well and is one of the most interesting sailing replicas yet built and a great credit to her owner. This photograph by Barry Pearce was taken immediately before her launch.

Bottom right: See page 12 for details.

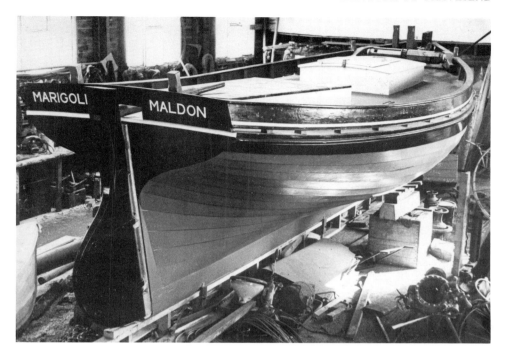

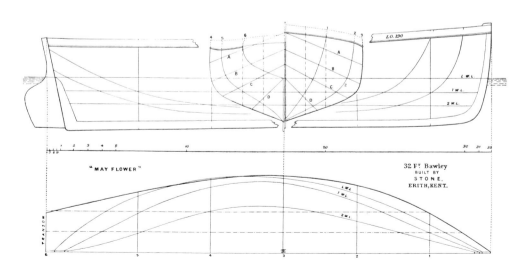

"MAY FLOWER"

32 F.T Bawley
BUILT BY
S T O N E,
ERITH, KENT.

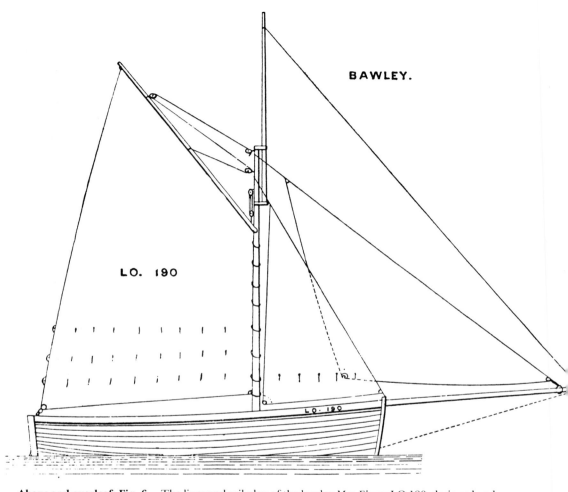

Above and overleaf: Fig. 6. The lines and sail plan of the bawley *May Flower* LO 180, designed and built by Douglas Stone at Erith, on the Thames, in the eighteen-eighties. The *May Flower* was a notably fast sailer, in keeping with young Douglas Stone's reputation as a designer of excellent yachts, fishing craft and sailing barges. He was born in 1860 and served an apprenticeship at the yacht and shipbuilding yard of John Harvey at Wivenhoe, Essex, before moving to Erith when he was twenty-one years old to start his own business, which was later removed to Brightlingsea.
The *May Flower*'s dimensions were 32 feet overall length by 11 feet 4 inches beam and 4 feet draught aft. Displacement was 13.3, tons of which 6 tons was internal ballast. Sail areas were: mainsail 394 square feet, jib 180 square feet, foresail 100 square feet; a total of 674 square feet without the jib-headed topsail. Stone's yard was probably the last to design and build a sailing smack—the little cutter *Peace* launched in 1909 for Stanley French of West Mersea. Like all craft turned out by Douglas Stone and his son Robert who succeeded him, the *Peace* was carefully designed on paper and working drawings, and all usual calculations for a small sailing vessel were made. This was a usual practice in most Colne yards in that and earlier times.

Fig. 7. The bawley LO 406 moored off Gravesend in the nineteen-thirties. She still carries a full rig, except for the bowsprit and jib, and the topmast is short, almost a chock pole. An iron hand capstan had been installed amidships to haul the trawl warp. Sweeps and a boathook are carried in lumber irons shipped on the port bulwark rail. A shrimp trawl hangs to dry from the masthead. In the background a gaggle of ship tugs lie at the buoys in Gravesend Reach.

Fig. 8.   This bow view of LO 406, taken at Gravesend, shows the full bow of the bawley and the fine ending of the bow waterlines, sweeping in to the stem from the powerful shoulders of the hull just forward of the mast; a characteristic of many bawleys but not found in such pronounced form in a smack.

CHAPTER TWO

The Medway

THE MEDWAY is the principal river of Kent, rising in the rural hinterland amid rolling countryside and flowing generally north-eastwards to join the estuary of the Thames to the north of the Isle of Sheppey. The reaches of the Medway just above and for some distance below Rochester became dominated by industry; cement making, brick making, and naval shipbuilding and repairing at the once great dockyards of Chatham and Sheerness. The lower reaches were frequently filled with traffic, both commercial and naval, with sailing barges predominating. Merchant steamships and warships of all sizes and types contributed to its hazards. However, despite traffic and pollution, lively fishing communities existed on the Medway, largely based on Rochester, Chatham and Strood. They used peter boats, bawleys and an occasional smack in their work and clung to the pointed-stern doble, a variant of the small peter boats of the Thames, into the twentieth century. The story of the men and their craft has been well told by Derek Combe in his book *The Bawleymen*.

The small, transom-sterned type of peter boat existed in the Medway at least as early as the beginning of the nineteenth century. A model of the spritsail-rigged Rochester boat *Pearl* is in the town museum. By the eighteen-twenties many were rigged with a gaff mainsail having a brail. We have the contemporary plans of a fast sailing peter boat taken from a boat built at Strood in about 1820. On dimensions of 27 foot 6 inches overall length, 9 foot 6 inches beam and 4 foot 2 inches draught aft and 2 foot 6 inches forward she carried a boomless cutter rig identical to that of the later bawleys. These boats were refined in hull form and this was noted on the plan made of this boat by an Admiralty draughtsman, who wrote "Particularly marked for her superior Sailing". She differed from the later bawleys in having the mast stepped through the deck to the keelson and by having a fish well amidships.

By the late nineteenth century the Medway bawleys were almost identical with those of Harwich and Leigh, though the draught was rather less. Most had the mast stepped in a wooden tabernacle to allow it to be lowered to pass Rochester bridge on the way up or down river during the smelt-fishing season. Medway bawleys usually had a bulkhead at the end of the fish hold, dividing it from the steering cockpit and separate from the after end of the long hatch. For some reason Essex bawleys did not have this sensible feature. The Medway bawleymen sailed in a winding and congested river and accordingly demanded good performance from their craft. Most were handy boats, and with the mainsail set a Medway bawley could be sailed by one man in most conditions.

The doble had most of the characteristics of the pointed-sterned, clinker-planked rowing and sailing Thames peter boat. It was about 18 to 20 feet long and was used for several types of fishing including smelt fishing, flue- and drag-netting and sometimes for towing a small beam trawl. Often rowed, it was also rigged with a sprit mainsail and a foresail, but most seem to have performed indifferently under sail. Surprisingly, dobles were still being built into the nineteen-twenties. The *Katie* was launched in 1907 and the last, a transom-sterned doble, was built in 1920. Some set lugsails instead of the spritsail and a few later boats had a daggerboard. Some bawley owners also had a doble for alternative forms of fishing.

The term doble was also used in the Essex Stour and in nearby Hamford Water to describe a rowing boat of shallow draught, used for fishing. It had a flat bottom, but the sides were shaped in section and were clinker-planked. The stem profile and the transom shape resembled that of a smack's boat, or a skiff. Although no photograph or drawing of these boats seems to exist, it seems likely they were of the same shape and perhaps origin as the "flatbottoms" of Cley, Blakeney and Wells on the north Norfolk coast. This type may have originated in Sweden and be very ancient: similar Swedish craft exist in use and are known as either "plattbonning" or "platteka", depending on use and district.

The Medway smelt fishery was one which set the river apart from other Kent and Essex activities. It often took place above Rochester, as far as the fishing boundary at Hawkwood, six miles upstream. These small, herring-like fish were a Victorian and Edwardian delicacy which have since disappeared. The smelts were found in various places in the Medway, in season and in varying numbers. They were taken with a form of peter net or seine net as a doble drifted with the tide. The spring was a good time for smelting and a bawley was often sailed upriver and was moored near the favourite grounds to provide accommodation for two or three doble-crews, while they fished for smelt. Sometimes they worked as a partnership, sharing out the returns each week.

Oysters had long been dredged in the Medway; this fact was recorded in the fifteen-sixties. This important fishery lasted until after the mid-nineteenth century under the supervision of the Medway Free Fishers, with various legislative restrictions, rights and duties. Spat and brood oysters were bought from Essex, Whitstable and elsewhere for re-laying on the grounds. Marketable oysters were sent to Billingsgate and the continent. Oyster dredging was a mainstay of the Medway fishermen until the severe winter of 1860–61 destroyed most of the stock and resulted in a long period of stagnation of cultivation by the Medway Freemen, despite several attempts to raise capital after the disastrous losses.

As a result some Medway oyster grounds were leased to merchants, some from local towns, others from Billingsgate and Essex. Gradually these new cultivators, who had money to invest, revived the oyster trade in the river and its creeks, employing some local fishermen. At that time an old Ramsgate smack, the *Sappho*, was moored in Captains Creek as a watch smack against theft from the grounds.

Bawleys and smacks continued to dredge Medway oysters under sail into the twentieth century. The trade revived considerably during the eighteen-nineties and some merchants imported foreign oysters for re-laying. Unfortunately increasing sewage and other pollution from the Medway towns adversely affected the oysters in the river, resulting in several poisoning incidents and closure of some grounds. However, the Freemen continued to dredge, as did the men employed by merchants. In 1922 a rich and unsuspected ground of oysters was accidentally discovered by a Freeman and very good money was made from it until it was worked out. It enabled several Medway bawley owners to have engines installed in their craft, and this allowed a bawley to dredge with a crew of two, instead of the three carried under sail. Medway oystering continued until the severe winter of 1939–40 which once more killed almost all the stock.

The Medway fishermen had faith in their craft and the future of their trade well into the twentieth century. The sailing bawley *Susannah* RR5 was built at Rochester in 1908 by the Co-operative Barge Society yard for John Hill, one of a line of Medway fishermen. Her dimensions were 39 foot overall length, 13 foot 3 inches beam and 5 foot 6 inches draught. She cost £210. John Hill was a progressive fisherman and had a 10 hp Victor petrol engine installed while building. There was much interest in engines by most fishermen at that time and those who could afford it were having them installed in many new and existing boats in several countries. The Medway bawleys were owned by individuals, like the Essex craft; they too were sometimes named after well known racing yachts contemporary with their date of build. *Alarm*, *Florinda*, *Thistle* and *Ivernia* were some of their names. Others were more homely such as *Dora*, *Clive*, *Francois*, *Lass of Kent*, *William and Elizabeth*. The bawleys turned to shrimping in the 1860s, when the oyster trade started to collapse. They worked the same type of trawl as the Leigh and Harwich men and fished in the Thames approaches and sometimes beyond, as far as the Wallet channel, off the north-east Essex coast.

A few Medway bawleys, the *Thistle*, *Ivernia*, *Olive* and *Francois*, with perhaps others, occasionally went stowboating for sprats in the Thames estuary, but this was regarded as dangerous work by their crews. Essex smacks often landed cargoes of sprats at various wharves in the Medway, and at least one Medway bawley, the *Jubilee*, sailed out to buy sprats from Essex smacks stowboating, for re-sale in the Medway.

Herrings, flatfish, eels, whitebait, crabs and lobsters were also taken at times in commercial quantities by the fishermen. Their way of life continued into the nineteen-thirties with only slow change and lingered on into the nineteen-forties on a reduced scale. These men, pacing the decks of their bawleys or rowing their dobles, were much fewer than their Essex counterparts but appear to have been equally resourceful and skilled at their fishing. Pocock, Raycraft, Hill, Wadhams, Underhill, Page and Williamson were some of their names.

Occasional races were held for the Medway sailing bawleys. In that of 1872 there were three classes: the first class for bawleys over 35 feet in length; second class for those of 32 feet and under 35 feet and third for those under 32 feet. The largest competing was the *William and Elizabeth*, owned by T. Germany, at 37 feet 6 inches, and the smallest was D. Williamson's *Victory* at 25 feet 10 inches. There were silver cups and cash prizes and much pride in their winning. The course sailed was from Strood pier out to the West Oaze, just below the Nore Sand, and back.

The difference in size of the bawleys racing showed the increase in dimensions over a period of about thirty years; fishing vessels in Essex and Kent increased considerably in size and quality between about 1845 and 1885. There were other bawley races on the Medway, including one in 1873 and another in 1889. There may have been others, but as elsewhere by the nineteen-twenties sail was in rapid decline. However, the Medway fishermen remained true to their bawleys and dobles into the mid-twentieth century and a few examples survive, kept in affection by their descendants and other enthusiasts.

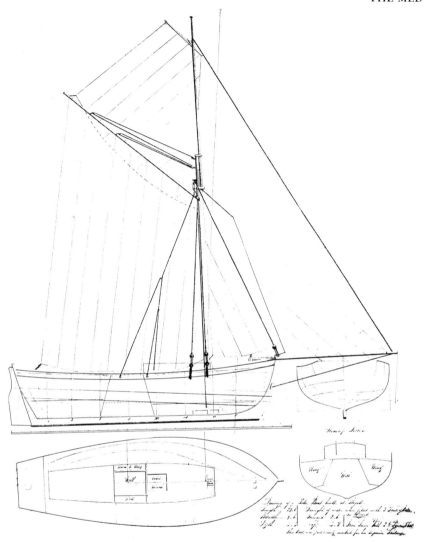

Fig. 9. Profile and sail plan of a 27 foot 6 inches transom-sterned peter boat built at Strood, on the Medway, about 1820. She carries the boomless cutter rig of the later bawleys and was a notably fast sailer. Her beam was 9 feet 6 inches and draught aft 4 feet 2 inches. A wet well was built into the hull amidships to keep fish alive while the craft was afloat. These wells in decked craft were usually in the form of a truncated pyramid, ending at the deck, in which was a hatch for access. The wooden well structure was caulked watertight and small holes were bored in the bottom planking to allow a free flow of water. The smaller cross-sectional area at the upper part of the trunk below the deck reduced the free surface effect on the stability of the boat. Wells were fairly common in many types of fishing craft until the mid-nineteenth century. Afterwards fishing patterns changed in many places, principally due to the effects of the railways on the carriage of fish to market.

19

Fig. 10. A Rochester bawley drawn by Robert C. Leslie in the late nineteenth century. Leslie was a shrewd observer of craft and we may be sure this drawing is thoroughly representative of a Medway bawley in the mid to late nineteenth century. The rig is typical of all sailing bawleys but the hull form, clinker planking, low freeboard amidships and the finely shaped transom reveal an earlier influence. The other interesting feature is the coach roof amidships, where the fish hold or shrimping well might be in later craft. The deck arrangement shown might well have been that of many mid-nineteenth-century bawleys before shrimping became commercially successful in the eighteen-sixties.

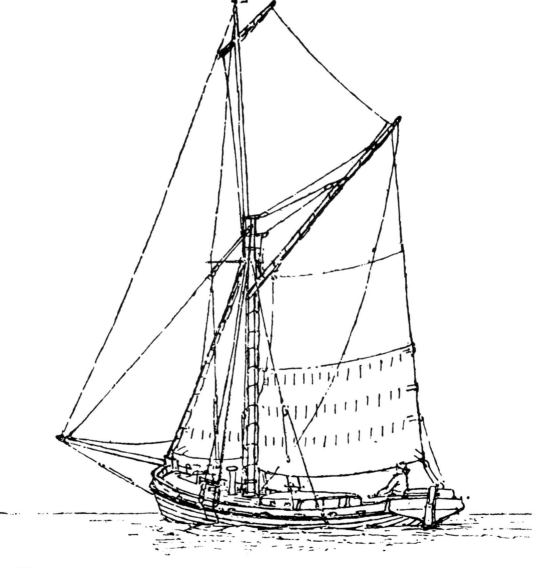

20

Fig. 11. The Medway bawley *Olive* reefed for working to control speed in a fresh breeze. Most Medway bawleys sailed well and were smartly handled in the relatively narrow and congested river.

Fig. 12. A tier of fishing bawleys in the Medway about 1928. Numbers of bawleys were owned on the river and moored at Rochester, Chatham, Strood and Queenborough. Many were built by Gill and Son at Rochester, the noted barge builders. Others were by E. Lemon of Strood. The bawley method of stowing the boomless mainsail by gathering it to the gaff with tyers and then hoisting the throat, leaving the peak on deck to run rain off, is shown here. Like the smacks, each bawley had a boat, usually known as a skiff (skift) and in earlier times as a foot boat. These were clinker-planked, 12 to 14 foot transom-sterned boats which withstood hard use. Bawleys lingered on the Medway almost as long as at Leigh but were gradually replaced by motor craft of shallower draught by the nineteen-fifties.

Fig. 13. John Hill's bawley *Susannah* RR 5 built in 1908, under motor and sail on the Medway in 1930. She was the last sailing bawley built for a Medway fisherman and the first to have a motor installed when built. The topmast is housed and a beam trawl, probably for shrimping, is carried to port. The length of the gaff and arrangement of the peak halyards were typical of a bawley.

Fig. 14. The bawley *Ivernia* at moorings off Strood in the early nineteen-sixties. This shows the beam and broad decks of a bawley compared to the proportionally narrower smacks, and the attractive shape of the stern. Her mast appears to have been slightly reduced in height, but a mainsail and foresail are still carried for emergency use. The small steering well forward of the tiller was typical of Medway bawleys but not usually found in those from Essex. Two other ex-sailing bawleys lie on a mooring beyond.

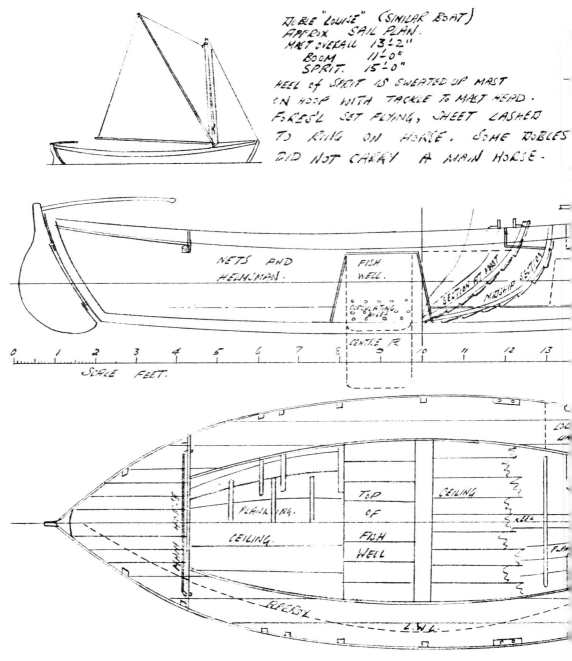

DOBLE "LOUISE" (SIMILAR BOAT)
APPROX SAIL PLAN.
MAST OVERALL 13'2"
BOOM 11'0"
SPRIT. 15'0"
HEEL OF SPRIT IS SWEATED UP MAST
ON HOOP WITH TACKLE TO MAST HEAD.
FORES'L SET FLYING, SHEET LASHED
TO RING ON HORSE. SOME DOBLES
DID NOT CARRY A MAIN HORSE.

NETS AND HELMSMAN.

FISH WELL.

CIRCULATING HOLES

CENTRE FR

SECTION OF MAST

MIDSHIP SECTION

0 1 2 3 4 5 6 7 8 9 10 11 12 13

SCALE FEET.

PLANKING.

CEILING.

TOP OF FISH WELL

CEILING

KEEL

FISH

MAIN HORSE

R.W'L.

L.W.L.

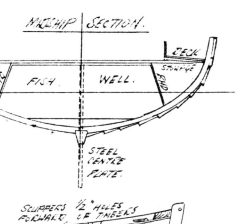

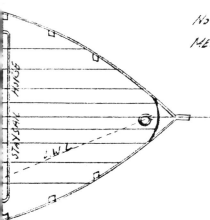

IN MARCH 1933 THERE WERE
17 DOBLES IN THE MEDWAY
FISHING BETWEEN ROCHESTER BRIDGE
AND RAINHAM, BUT ONLY ABOUT 3
CARRIED SAIL.

SOME DOBLES CARRIED NO CENTRE
PLATE.

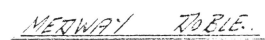

MEDWAY DOBLE.

R.R. 28. OWNER FRED. J. WADHAMS.
LINES TAKEN OFF AT STROOD PIER 1933.

NO SAIL PLAN TAKEN BUT SPRIT
MEASURED 14'-10" S.A.

Overleaf/previous pages and below: Fig. 15.   The pointed-sterned, clinker-planked fishing doble of the Medway was a direct relation or derivative of the Thames peter boat. Typical dimensions were 18 to 19 feet overall with a 6 to 6 foot 6 inch beam. The planking was usually oak on sawn-oak frames and the heavy hulls had the advantage of carrying way when the nets were being worked. A doble had a wet well, the deck being set below the sheer, and there were drain scuppers as in the Thames peter boats. Like the peter boats a doble could be sailed with a sprit-mainsail and a small foresail, or could be rowed. Some later ones had a dagger plate to aid windward sailing, but most made do without. Most dobles were built by Albert Lemon of Strood or Gill of Rochester.

The dobles were much used for netting smelt and flounder and occasionally towed a small trawl or oyster dredge. Many were owned by men who also owned a bawley, and the larger boat then served as accommodation when, for example, the owner was smelt fishing in the river.

The *May* was the last Medway doble to be afloat and she is seen here alongside the Medway bawley *Ivernia* at Strood in the early nineteen-seventies, fitted for an outboard motor. Since 1984 she has been preserved, with her rig and equipment, at the Medway Heritage Centre.

CHAPTER THREE

The Oyster Dredgers of Whitstable

THE TOWN of Whitstable, on the north shore of Kent, faces the estuary of the Thames. It is just east of the Isle of Sheppey and the eastern entrance of the Swale, the narrow channel which separates Sheppey from the mainland of Kent. In its heyday at the beginning of the twentieth century Whitstable was a comparatively isolated town of about 7,000 inhabitants. Its foreshore and that at nearby Reculvers has been an oyster ground since before Roman times. Oysters have been gathered there for centuries.

As with many oyster fisheries the rights of those at Whitstable, on land and in the water, passed into the ownership of commoners during the late eighteenth century. At that time Viscount Bolingbroke, as Lord of the Manor, sold to "Thomas Ford of Seasalter, Mariner, and William Smith of Seasalter, shipwright, . . . the Manor of Whitstable, . . . and also all the fishing of Whitstable, being a royalty fishery or oyster dredging".

They sold it again, parting the land and water interests. The "Sea Manor" was bought by Thomas Ford who at once re-sold it.

Long before these transactions occurred Whitstable men who dredged for oysters associated as the "Ancient Company of Dredgers". They worked the grounds as tenants of the Lord of the Manor. In 1793 they had the chance to break free: funds were raised for a company and an act of parliament allowed establishment of The Company of Free Fishers and Dredgers of Whitstable, with a capital of £20,000 and the right to appoint their own officers.

Reeves, Kemp and Ougham were among the old Whitstable fishing families and featured in the records of the Whitstable Oyster Fishery Company. This company bought the rights to an area of oyster ground off the town and operated as a company of freemen, managed by a foreman, a deputy foreman and a jury of twelve members who were elected annually. In this it much resembled the constitution of the old Colchester Oyster Fishery Company. It also suffered from the same problems in that the freemen were, apprenticed to the company, at first at sixteen years old and later at twenty-one. Finally, as the numbers of freemen grew, the privilege was restricted to the eldest son of a freeman. Even then, the numbers were too great to be absorbed in the work of the Whitstable oyster fishery and many had to find alternative employment.

The craft used to dredge oysters from Whitstable were of two types during the eighteenth and nineteenth centuries. Many, particularly until the late nineteenth century, were transom-sterned, bawley-style cutters having brailing mainsails and considerable beam, like the bawleys from Leigh and Harwich. The other type were counter-sterned cutter smacks similar to those from Essex but having generally less draught and fuller sections. Before about 1850 many had only short cheeks forward and aft, with an open well amidships.

The transom-sterned Whitstable bawleys were about 32–38 feet in length. Many of these were also owned at the small ports on the Swale. Some of these craft had a boom and gaff mainsail and some set a standing lug mizzen on a mast stepped at the transom. The lug was sheeted to a long outrigger and the rig was reputedly shipped in season for herring drifting, but photographs show it in use with trawl beams on deck. It is just possible that this rig was the origin of the term "Whitstable yawl", but I think it most unlikely. The term yawl was also used on the River Blackwater for sailing fishing vessels in the eighteenth century and may then have particularly referred to dredging craft. These bawleys set large topsails and altogether expose the fallacy of attempting to catalogue types of craft too closely.

The cutter smacks which evolved at Whitstable were of a form and size similar to the Essex smacks. Many were built at Whitstable, often in yards owned and operated by fishery companies. Most were designed by the yard foreman. The *Czarina* F 131 was built in 1845, and her dimensions are interesting as probably being typical of the size of Whitstable smacks at the time, which seem, like those from other places, to have been smaller than they became later in the century. The *Czarina* had a 36 foot waterline length with 10 foot beam and 5 foot depth of hold. The length of keel was 30 feet. She was acquired by the Seasalter and Ham Oyster Fishery Company in 1879. Like many smacks and bawleys of her time the *Czarina* was built with clinker planking. Later this was doubled, and after some years a further skin was fitted to strengthen the old hull, and she emerged with the external appearance of carvel planking.

Many of the late nineteenth and early twentieth century Whitstable smacks were designed by a local man, John Morday, and were built at yards in the town owned either by the oyster companies or by individuals. Some were built at Whitstable by Richard and Charles Perkins, who launched *Stormy Petrel* in 1899 for the Seasalter and Ham Oyster Company. Like many Whitstable smacks she had a rather square and box-like counter, which was ideal for her work in dredging oysters. In 1928 she became a watch boat for the Company grounds on the Pollard Spit. After a days' dredging, the crew of a watch boat was expected to be alert at night, at anchor, for any illegal dredging or the theft of oysters from the grounds. The crew manned the watch smack for fourteen days at a time, then another smack took over the task. Although she appears a bulky vessel, the dimensions are not large for a smack. On a length of 40 feet, her beam of 13 feet 9 inches gives a greater proportion of beam to length than in many smacks, and her draft of 5 feet 9 inches is moderate. She is, at 12 registered tons, rated as a smack of the second class, the lower limit of which starts at 15 tons. She is a powerful and in some ways an unusually romantic-looking craft.

Whitstable smacks were almost all rigged as cutters, though a very few later ones were ketches. The hulls had fuller bilges and not so much rise of floor as the Essex smacks. This was to facilitate their taking the ground off Whitstable when at moorings. For the same reason their bottom construction was strong; the Whitstable foreshore is generally hard, and when lifting to a tide or when taking the ground in strong winds and rough water the Whitstable smacks inevitably received a pounding.

The cutter-rigged *Rose and Ada* was a typical Whitstable smack with dimensions of 46 foot 8 inches length from the fore side of stem to the end of a rather angular and flat-sectioned counter. Waterline length was 40 feet 8 inches and the draughts 5 feet 8 inches aft and 4 feet forward. The smack rig was the usual gaff cutter, but in many the mast seems to have been stepped further forward than in cutter smacks from other places. Usually four rectangular ports were cut in the bulwark in way of the dredgermen's stations, allowing ready disposal of unwanted shell and rubbish from the deck during dredging.

The term yawl was applied to many of these craft, as it had been in earlier times to similar boats in the Essex Blackwater. There is no evidence that the Whitstable craft carried a yawl rig, other than the possibility of a link with the bawley-style dredging boats of the district, which often stepped a mizzen on which a lugsail was set. The term possibly referred to clinker-planked craft, which most Whitstable dredging boats were into the mid nineteenth century. Originally they may have been undecked. However, a deck is so desirable for oyster dredging and trawling that it is probable they were decked long before the eighteenth century. When dredging, the Whitstable smacks and bawleys were used in work which allowed the crews to get home at night, except for occasional short trips. Most boats had locker berth accommodation in the fo'c'sle. The larger smacks had a cabin aft, like the Essex smacks of that size, with four berths around the cabin sides, each entered through a small opening which could be closed by sliding shutters. There were locker seats before the berths and a water tank and a coal stove completed the furnishings. In these craft the fo'c'sle was used as a store.

A Whitstable smack worked a fleet usually consisting of six dredges, three being towed from each side of the smack. The two heaviest dredges were towed from forward, two medium ones from amidships and the lightest ones aft. The iron dredges were of the same A-framed type used by the Essex smacks, with a hoeing edge, a chain mesh bottom and a net back and sides spread by a stick at the end. The weight of these dredges was about 22–28 pounds each. They were towed on bass warps which had a wooden buoy made fast at the end. The other end was bent on to the ring at the head of the dredge. The force of towing was taken by a rope stopper from the rigging, made fast to the warp by a rolling hitch. If the dredge fouled, or the stopper parted and the dredgerman could not hold the warp, the buoy was cast over and the dredge was recovered later. Dredges were hauled by hand and were emptied on deck before being again cast overboard. The dredgermen then culled the oysters from the mass of weed, crabs, stones, mud and other rubbish on deck, retaining the marketable oysters or those to be re-laid on the grounds. The rubbish was shaded overboard.

Although by custom and preference Whitstable smacks and bawleys laid to moorings on the foreshore, close to their work on the oyster grounds, the town had a tidal harbour, which had existed for many years but was small and shallow. However, by the eighteen-twenties the merchants of Canterbury and businessmen of the surrounding district were pressing for the expansion of the harbour in conjunction with the construction of a railway line to link their city with the Thames estuary for increasing trade not only to London but other countries. The railway was built between Canterbury and Whitstable in 1830 and was the first in the world to carry passengers as well as goods. As a result an improved and enlarged harbour was built at Whitstable in 1834 and soon served a variety of ships and cargoes from many places and countries. Although it was sometimes used by fishing vessels its confines and charges resulted in most of the Whitstable fishing fleet continuing to lie on the exposed foreshore.

The large areas of oyster beds off Whitstable were divided into sections for oysters at various stages of growth; spat, brood, half ware, and ware. Each stage takes about twelve months, so that to produce a native oyster fit for eating takes five to six years. As oysters spawn in summer, a close season on dredging is observed from May until September. During this time brood oysters are taken to fattening beds and grounds are dredged to clear them of five-fingers (starfish) oyster-drills and crabs, which are the principal pests.

Besides the freemen, other local fishermen were employed by the companies to clear grounds, and they also dredged on the public oyster ground for brood and half-ware oysters, for sale to the Company of Free Fishers. These men were known as flatsmen, as their work was principally on the Kentish flats.

In 1867 there were 408 Free Dredgermen, including the widows of former members, who retained their husbands' status. Of this number about three hundred were working members; the oyster trade was a mainstay at Whitstable, with eighty or so sailing smacks working the grounds off the town and in the nearby Swale and adjacent waters, with occasional voyages to other oyster areas for stock. A few of the larger smacks from Whitstable also seem to have engaged in dredging for oysters off the Dutch coast and in the English Channel at times during the nineteenth century.

Only a proportion of the freemen were required to man the smacks and gradually a class of non-fishing freemen emerged who had other occupations. They received a one-third share of any profits of the company. Widows and the sick were also cared for by the company, which, rightly, had high standing locally.

The Whitstable men had always a sense of rivalry with the Essex oystermen and fishermen. Despite this for centuries there was a lively trade between them in oysters, and Essexmen frequently fished the north Kent coast for sprats and dredged five fingers there for manure. As the Whitstable fishermen did not usually have to sail far from their moorings for work the far-ranging Essex smacksmen regarded them as "stay at homes". This unfortunate attitude did not help relations between men with similar interests and good qualities.

As most of the Kentish shore was common ground it was visited by scores of smacks from Essex which dredged brood and other oysters there, often to the annoyance of the Kentish oystermen. The earliest recorded instance of this occurred in 1598. Smacks from the Colne and Blackwater rivers were often there on oyster business and also came to dredge young oysters, frequently delivering the catch to the Whitstable Oyster Company. They then used the Swale in numbers as an anchorage. Nevertheless a rivalry, usually subdued, remained between the Essex and Kent fishermen until the end of fishing under sail.

In the summer of 1901 there was a heavy fall of spat (young oysters) and this was especially prolific on the Kent shore off Bishopstone, where the Kentish fishermen were making the most of the harvest. Unfortunately the weather settled to a hard easterly wind and the best ground was surrounded by rocks and boulder banks, all making it difficult work. Nevertheless, it was only a few days, as the local historian Collard put it, before "some deep-keeled Colchester smacks slammed in alongside the flatsmen and worked until high-tide, hauling their dredges up through 24 feet of water. They delivered their catch to the company's store, amounting to ten washes per boat for one tide's work, and Whitstable people said they had never before seen so much brood delivered, stacked up as it was like a haystack".

In 1880 another oyster company was formed at Whitstable, known as The Seasalter and Ham Oyster Fishery. This bought oyster beds to the west of the free fishers' grounds and smacks to work them. The great demand for oysters allowed both companies to operate with little risk of interference in each other's markets.

Seasalter and Ham, as this company became known, owned two principal oyster grounds: the Pollard of 500 acres and the Ham of 1,200 acres. These were divided into squares of about five acres each, known as grounds. The grounds were numbered and were marked with buoys having numbered flags. Grounds used for fattening each supported about a quarter of a million oysters, and when the season started in September the smacks were given orders to dredge various grounds defined by the numbers. Six or eight smacks might be seen methodically dredging across an allotted ground until the quota to be taken that day according to the foreman was achieved. The oysters were taken ashore in sacking bags and were washed and graded on culling tables, usually into five grades. These were packed into barrels for despatch, and were usually sent by rail to Billingsgate fishmarket in London. Dredging continued through autumn and winter, until ending in April.

During the close season from May to September, many of the smacks' crews were employed in maintaining and renewing the beacons marking the oyster beds and in overhauling the heavy moorings laid for the smacks. These were made fast to a chain which was secured to a large iron "corkscrew"; this was turned into the bottom on the exposed shore at low water. During the close season the smacks were sent in turn to the company's yard or elsewhere for refitting. Others continued dredging for oyster pests and might also transfer some oyster stocks on the grounds, besides dredging specified areas to keep them clean for oyster-laying.

As with the Colne Fishery company, there were ceremonies at Whitstable to mark the opening of the oyster season. A large smack, such as the *Seasalter*, was used for this. Her scrubbed deck was crowded with directors, fish buyers, hoteliers and other principal customers out for a day's sail, with food and drink to celebrate the hauling of the first dredge of the season, which invariably came up well filled.

Like all oyster fisheries the Whitstable grounds had watch smacks, as oyster theft was much more common than is perhaps now realised. The smacks *Stormy Petrel* RR 23, built as late as 1910 and now a yacht, and the *Three Brothers* were regular watch smacks.

Gradually the numbers of freemen of the Company of Free Fishers became impossible to manage and in 1896 the concern was reconstructed as a public company with a nominal capital of £250,000, then a very large sum. Each member of the company was allotted twenty £10 shares. A board of directors was established and a secretary was appointed in place of the old office of Treasurer. A storesman was appointed to supervise the oyster depot and also a foreman with responsibility for dredging operations by the smacks. He was the most important employee. A water bailiff collected the anchorage and other dues for the company.

At the time these changes took place there was a remarkable fall of oyster spat, in 1900 and 1901. Prospects seemed good for the new venture, and oyster cultivation at Whitstable by the two companies continued evenly. The grounds were dredged by the many smacks, and activities ashore matched those afloat. However, the outbreak of war in 1914 disrupted the industry seriously; like most other things in Britain, it was never to be the same again. Many of the oystermen were Naval Reserve men or volunteered for the Navy. Others served elsewhere, many in merchant ships. The oyster grounds were left almost unattended for four years.

After the war cultivation was resumed. By the early nineteen-twenties there were fourteen smacks working for the Seasalter and Ham Oyster Fishery

Company, of which the 65 foot *Seasalter* was the largest. She was built at Whitstable in 1875 for the company, principally to carry oysters to and from her home port. She voyaged to Falmouth, Brittany, Holland and Belgium before 1914 and in her early years may well have dredged oysters off the Dutch coast at times, and possibly down Channel.

The *Seasalter* was also used to dredge on the Whitstable grounds and often carried oysters from the Essex rivers Crouch, Roach and Blackwater for re-laying on the Whitstable beds. Her crew were paid a weekly wage, and it seems that very few Whitstable smacks were owned by individual fishermen as was usual in Essex.

By the early nineteen-twenties the *Seasalter* was making weekly trips all the year round to the Essex rivers for loads of oysters, but she also usually dredged the Whitstable grounds for the first three days of the week in season. An old trade of bringing cargoes of oyster barrels from Belgium was kept up by the *Seasalter* at that time. These barrels were known locally as kits. She was sometimes sailed by a crew of three men but should have had four. Her skipper at that time was a young Whitstable man named Albert Stroud who ably carried on the local seafaring traditions.

The *Seasalter* was reasonably fast and once made three consecutive round trips to the East Scheldt for Dutch oysters, sailing in spring weather conditions. She brought home a total of two million oysters in the three trips, to be relaid at Whitstable. The last was to be her final foreign voyage.

A new peril threatened the Whitstable oyster industry by the early nineteen-twenties, when a disease affected the grounds. It was also rife on the Continent and everywhere losses were high. It became so serious that scientists were brought in and the Seasalter and Ham company engaged forty smacks to dredge the grounds and clear the many dead oysters, landing the shell to be bleached in the sun for further use as culch. As the mortality worsened many smacks were laid up and were sold for conversion to yachts. The *Sydney*, built at Whitstable in 1828, was hulked by the company as a boundary mark between their grounds and those adjoining. The old *Czarina* was sold to a West Mersea fisherman for £12 and was towed there by the *Seasalter* on one of her oyster-carrying voyages to the Blackwater.

By the autumn of 1920 about half of the Whitstable oysters had died. This rose to three quarters of the stock by the following year and resulted in a reduction of wages for the smacks' crews of both oyster companies. Some fishermen found other work, in merchant ships, in factories or as hands on yachts. Soon the larger smacks became redundant, and few wished to sail in them because of the weight of the gear for a small crew. Eventually these were laid-up and were sold or broken up, the *Seasalter* among them, still sound and fit for sea.

The disease passed. The Seasalter and Ham company retrenched and bought new stock from France. A slow recovery was achieved, but in 1929 a severe winter killed vast numbers of oysters; prospects were again bleak. The company strove to survive, and to improve efficiency engines were installed in several smacks to ensure regularity in dredging, whatever the wind. More new stock was purchased, but the demand for oysters was slowly falling, aided by the depression in trade and the emergence of the oyster as a luxury food, in contrast to its Victorian image. Many men left the Whitstable oyster fleet for more secure employment and once again some smacks were laid up, eventually to be sold to become yachts.

In 1939 war disrupted the industry and the grounds were neglected. By 1946 there were only eight smacks remaining, all with engines. Again the Seasalter and Ham restored cultivation and also bought grounds at Falmouth in Cornwall, to spread their risks. Work continued fairly evenly for some years until the severe winter of 1962–63, which shattered most east-coast oyster cultivation. The company survived but with only two smacks, the *Rose and Ada* and the *Speedwell*. Mortality of stock was very high and industrial pollution in the area was contributing to the rapid decline, and in 1964 the purchase of the Seasalter and Ham company by Associated Fisheries took place. After a period of experimental development a new company was formed 1972 named Seasalter Shelfish, to exploit the artificial rearing of oysters on a large scale at Whitstable and for growing them under scientific control in the Swale and Medway. This is a new and fascinating story, but the days of dredging oysters by sailing smack are long gone.

Opposite page, top: Fig. 16. Four Whitstable smacks reefed down for dredging on the oyster grounds. This shows the broad counters of the Whitstable cutters, which were strongly built for oyster dredging and needed the maximum deck space aft of the mast. Working on what was often a weather shore and in local waters most of the time, these cutters developed features denied to smacks, which were expected to have multiple-purpose use in spratting, fish trawling, oyster and five-finger dredging, and salvaging when necessary. The Whitstable smacks were built with especially strong bottom structure to withstand settling on and lifting from the exposed local foreshore at each tide, which with the wind "on" could be rough and punishing to a wooden vessel.

Fig. 17. Whitstable smacks manoeuvring under sail in a fresh wind. As several carry a topsail this picture was probably taken before the start of a regatta race.

Fig. 18. Port bow view of the Whitstable smack F 76 in use for pleasure sailing, lying in Whitstable harbour about 1959. This gives an excellent view of the deck arrangements. The bowsprit is run in through the bitts. The ratlines on the shrouds are probably not original.

Fig. 19. A view of the deck of Whitstable smack F 76 showing the square style of counter that was typical of these craft, the mainsheet arrangements, which differed from those generally used in Essex smacks, the breadth of deck carried well aft to provide space for dredging, and the length of gaff and bowsprit.
The craft alongside is one of the 35 to 40 foot motor fishing boats owned at Whitstable in the nineteen-fifties which were much used for pair trawling for sprats with a Larsen net—the device which superseded stowboating on the Essex and Kent coast after the nineteen-forties.

Above: Fig. 20. Bawleys from Faversham Creek, in Kent, worked from this small port off the Swale. The bawley with white sails in the background of the photograph is rigged in the typical fashion of the late nineteenth century. The Faversham-registered bawley in the foreground, FM 113, carries the rig of an earlier time with a long-yarded, mid-nineteenth-century-style topsail and a standing lug mizzen sheeted to a long outrigger. This rig appears to have been common in the Swale bawleys in the nineteenth century and possibly earlier.

Luggers were built and owned at Margate, further east along the north coast of Kent; these were two- or three-masted craft, with a mizzen sheeted to an outrigger. As Margate was much used by bawleys from the Swale, Medway and sometimes also from Leigh, it is tempting to wonder if this hybrid rig was influenced by the Margate luggers. More probably it found some special application for a certain fishery or method of working; alternatively it provided more sail area for trawling, as this bawley carries a beam trawl with a large trawl head visible beyond her quarter. The last bawley working from Margate, the century-old *Providence*, still carried a mizzen in 1939.

Below: Fig. 21. The *Rose and Ada* ready for dredging with two reefs in the mainsail, staysail and a small jib set part way along the bowsprit to balance the rig. The topmast is housed. Her crew of six stand ready and she is surging along, despite short canvas for working, in a fresh breeze off Whitstable. Note ports in the bulkwarks for disposal of culch, a feature found only in smacks from Whitstable and the Swale.

Above: Fig. 22. The hull of the Whitstable oyster smack *Rose and Ada*, F 105, taken in 1970 at Greenhithe. The typical bow shape and counter of the Whitstable smacks is shown. Note the wash ports in the bulwarks for clearing the culch overboard and draining the deck of water. The mast was originally stepped through the deck and not in a tabernacle as shown in the illustration.

Below: Fig. 23. The clipper-bowed motor oyster dredger *Speedwell* was built by William King of Burnham on Crouch, Essex, for Smith Brothers, oyster merchants of Burnham in 1908. She is believed to have been the first British motor oyster dredger and was fitted with a Dan 18 hp paraffin engine. She was launched without a rig but was afterwards given a gaff ketch sailplan. Because of the motor the *Speedwell* could be worked by only three men and she attracted considerable interest when new.

After 1919 she was sold to The Seasalter and Ham Oyster Fishery Company at Whitstable and was re-engined but retained the ketch rig. After many years' working from Whitstable she was sold for conversion to a yacht.

This photograph was taken when the *Speedwell* was being refitted at the yard of Anderson, Rigden and Perkins, Whitstable, in 1933.

Fig. 24. Oyster dredging on board the Whitstable smack *Gamecock*, F 19, 1933, one of the last working the grounds.

Fig. 25. Whitstable smacks dredging oysters around 1900. The Whitstable smacks were built locally and had less sheer than their Essex counterparts and often more freeboard aft, which was surprising in craft intended almost exclusively for dredging. This smack appears to be about 50 feet long, but seems to have relatively light mast and spars for her size. This photograph was taken in summer, possibly when the smacks were clearing the grounds, as oysters are not dredged for sale in the period from May to September. This smack has the old form of counter, which was rectangular in plan and steeply raking in profile. The mast is sprung well forward and an old-fashioned yard topsail is set.

CHAPTER FOUR

The Leigh Bawleys

LEIGH lies on the foreshore of the north bank of the Lower Thames, adjacent to the equally old Essex village of Hadleigh and four miles upstream from Southend, a seaside resort beloved of Londoners and others since Victorian times, whose population growth and suburbs have gradually over-run the surrounding waterside districts of Chalkwell and Westcliff and spread eastwards to Shoebury, via Thorpe Bay, to form a conurbation with the population of a city. All this was far off when sailing bawleys lay in Leigh Creek and on the adjoining foreshore, when the old village of Leigh clustered along the High Street running narrow and parallel with the creek, with brick and weatherboarded houses lining its sides and alleys. Steam trains of the London, Tilbury and Southend Railway rumbled through the village on the line from Fenchurch Street Station in London to Shoebury. They brought the trippers with their demand for shrimp teas and other sea food and also took away many shrimps, oysters and other catches to Billingsgate and a variety of markets.

Shrimps were a staple catch of the Leigh bawleys from early Victorian times and possibly before. They were still being landed in quantities in the early nineteen-fifties but the supply has since diminished. Generally brown shrimps were found within a line from Walton Naze, cutting the Gunfleet Sand, the Middle Sunk and the Shingles shoals, towards Herne Bay on the north Kent coast. Eastward of that line was regarded as pink shrimp ground.

In Elizabethan times Leigh was described as "A proper haven . . . with a good store of lusty seamen". It seems always to have been the home of fishermen, but we know little of the early craft except that in common with all the Thames from London downstream the clinker-planked, pointed-stern small fishing boat known as a peter boat was in use for some time before the eighteenth century as a rowing and sailing boat, as described in chapter one. It seems that larger variants of the peter boat type were built for fishing in the Thames Estuary and the channels of the Essex coast. These were smaller than the early cutter smacks that developed for the same purpose.

Many peter boats were owned at Leigh. In the early nineteenth century, as elsewhere on the lower Thames, the larger peter boats retained the spritsail rig and with increasing size became known as pinks, from the pointed stern.

Leigh peter nets averaged 20 fathoms in length, 42 to 45 meshes deep, with mesh sizes varying from $3\frac{1}{4}$ to $3\frac{3}{4}$ inches, a few preferring 4 inches to catch larger flatfish. Petering, as such netting was called at Leigh, usually meant setting the net across a creek or a "swim" across the sands. The commencement of the flood tide outside was a preferred time, as there was then little current in the swim. A buoyed anchor was let go near one edge of the channel and the peter boat rowed to the other side, paying out the anchor ropes fastened to the ends of the top and bottom ropes of the net, which was then also paid out. Its other end was similarly bridled and anchored near the other shore so as to form a wall of mesh across the channel, into which the fish would swim. Sometimes other nets were set some distance above and below the first.

The fishermen then rowed back parallel to and a short distance from the lines of the headropes, beating the water with an ash pole to drive fish into the net. On reaching the other side one hand lifted the net buoy and anchor while the other rowed the boat ahead slowly as the net was hauled into the boat, its top and bottom brought together to form a bag and prevent fish escaping. When there was no flow of tide the fishermen "tinkled" the fish by jingling eight or so three-inch diameter iron rings, strung loosely on a bight at the end of a piece of line lowered to the bottom and bounced up and down as the boat was rowed across the nets. This disturbed the fish from the bottom, where they bury themselves at low water.

Besides the usual net fisheries, some pinks sailed down to the Maplin Sands off the flat shore of Foulness Island to set trot lines for flatfish with hooks made from thorns, pegged down to the sands at low water. This was called "sanding". Flatfish were also taken alongshore from Leigh to the Maplins with peter nets. The catches were transferred from the wet wells to store pits at Leigh from which, every two weeks, they were hauled by drag net and loaded into the wells of carrying peter boats which sailed them upriver to be sold at Billingsgate. Pinks were fully decked, with a small, low cabin top, and usually set a sprit mainsail with a topsail overset on a topmast, and a staysail and jib set on a bowsprit of modest length. There was no windlass for the anchor cable.

These craft worked mainly between the Nore Sand and Holehaven at the upper end of Sea Reach, on Canvey Island. Pinks had small wet wells amidships, bulkheaded from the small cabin forward and the hold aft. Like all such wells these ran the full width of the hull as far up as the waterline, then rose in a tapered trunk so that the free surface area of the water in them did not adversely affect stability.

A coloured lithograph by W. H. Timms entitled *Off Miffin Land* (plate 85) illustrates mid-nineteenth-century shipping in the Thames estuary and shows a sprit-rigged pink or large peter boat in the centre foreground. She has what appears to be a carvel-planked hull and is rigged with a boomed sprit mainsail with a loose foot, a staysail, jib and a topsail set on the pole masthead. The detail and feeling of the craft drawn suggest that they were accurately observed rather than drawn from fancy, and the peter boat represents a size and rig well suited to the estuary and capable of coastal fishing in fine weather.

About 1830 the *King William IV* was launched as the first Leigh peter boat with a transom stern. Only half a dozen were built during the next ten years, but gradually the pinks and peter boats were replaced by the transom-sterned peter boats of the type which were also evolving upriver at Greenwich and elsewhere and these seem to have developed into the powerful gaff-rigged bawleys. The last Leigh peter boat was fishing for eels in 1902 and the type is now remembered there only by the name of a well-known pub.

The bawley began to emerge in more or less its final form early in the nineteenth century. The plans of a Medway example are shown in the chapter on the bawleys of the Medway (fig. 10). Early examples from Leigh seem to have been half-decked boats fitted with a fish well, like their predecessors the smaller peter boats. By the eighteen-fifties the boats had increased in size and were fully decked. In those early days the Leigh bawleys went long-lining for cod and other fish, often taking the catch alive in the well to London's Billingsgate fish market. They also trawled for shrimps, which were landed at Leigh to be cooked in coppers ashore, before despatch to market or sale by local vendors. Stephen Frost is credited with starting the local shrimping trade in 1830. It brought a major part of its living to Leigh for over a century.

The early Leigh shrimpers used a type of small primitive trawl. This evolved into a triangular net with its mouth spread by a beam about 9 feet long which was towed along the bottom by a trawl warp and bridle. The mouth was extended by a vertical post about 18–24 inches high in the centre of the beam and this had a light horizontal beam, shorter than the lower beam, at its top, forming a quadrilateral mouth. As the size of the bawleys increased the boats towed more than one net, thus not increasing the labour of recovering each, but increasing their catching power. This method developed until by the eighteen-nineties a 35 foot bawley usually worked four nets, two boomed out from the hull abaft the mast and the others towed from the sides.

In 1850 one of the Cotgrove family of Leigh is reputed to have put a brick-built boiling copper in the hold of his bawley *Secret*, to boil the catch on board while fishing, enabling the shrimps to be landed ready for market. The term boiler may possibly have been the source of the term bawley. Another explanation is that the term once meant "large" in local usage; this might follow in the term "bawley boat", meaning a larger craft than the little pointed-sterned peter boats and the pinks once used at Leigh, or the slightly larger transom-sterned boats that were still known as peter boats into the mid-nineteenth century.

Eventually the mass of gear associated with the small beam nets sometimes known as trim trams was replaced by a single ordinary beam trawl with fine-mesh net. This was recovered by hand power, the mass of the catch being shaken out on deck, often filling it to the rails. While the bawley had another tow her crew sieved and sorted the catch, which was then boiled in the copper in the hold, ladled out, and spread to dry on netting supported by light battens between the coamings and the bulwark rail. The cooked, crisp shrimps were packed into pad baskets with sacking sewn over the tops before being labelled for the train.

The sailing bawley as finally evolved and built at Brightlingsea, Harwich, Leigh, Southend and on the river Medway and the Swale was powerful in hull form and rig. A typical boat built during the twenty years before 1914 varied between 35 and 42 feet in length overall, a 35-footer having 12 to 15 foot beam and 5 foot or 5 foot 6 inches draught. The hull had a straight keel, a straight stem, slightly rounded at the forefoot, and a transom stern with a slight rake but of surprisingly delicate shape in many boats. The sheer was high forward and swept down to little freeboard aft, though not so markedly as in the finer-lined Essex smacks.

The bawley hull had a very hollow entrance, as the shape was exaggerated by her beam, and this resulted in bold shoulders in way of the mast and usually considerable shape in the powerful hull sections, which, with the ample beam, made a bawley a stiffer sail carrier in smooth water than a smack of the same waterline length. Construction was strong and inexpensive, with sawn-oak frames, beams and centreline structure, pitch-pine bottom planking and pine side planking, deck and spars. They had low bulwarks and a thick oak wale strake belted the sheer. All the six or seven tons of iron ballast was carried in the bilge and was ceiled over. Below deck a bawley was arranged with accommodation so that for short periods four could live in the fo'c'sle, which usually extended aft of the mast and was entered by a hatch in the deck to starboard. The crew slept on the locker tops or in pipe cots above them and cooked on a coal stove. The hold occupied the remaining after space. In a shrimping bawley it was divided from forward into a net and gear store-room, space for the shrimp-boiling copper and general stowage of the catch and finally a steering well or space. The hold was served by a long, narrow and tapering hatch which had wooden covers for bad weather. This left wide side decks for working trawl or stowboat gear and for sorting a catch. A handspike windlass with a pawl-post was fitted across the foredeck, and many boats had a geared hand winch or wink mounted on a post amidships, to haul in the trawl warps.

The boomless cutter rig was the bawley's most distinctive feature. The mast was rather short, but a long fidded topmast was stepped and in a 35 foot boat the topmast head would be about 48 foot above the deck. Standing rigging comprised two shrouds a side, the foremost in line with the mast and the after 2 foot 6 inches or so further aft, with single topmast shrouds passing over the wooden spreaders and set up midway between the lower shrouds. A forestay led to the stemhead, and the two fish tackles for handling nets could be, and occasionally were, set up as backstays in heavy weather. The bowsprit stood about 17 foot 6 inches outboard, without shrouds, but had a running bobstay and a topmast stay.

The sail plan was tall and comparatively narrow but was efficient and handy to those accustomed to it. A 36-footer would set a mainsail of 500 square feet, referred to by many bawleymen as the trysail, a 200 square foot topsail, a 95 square foot stay foresail (staysail) and a 117 square foot working jib, the rig totalling 972 square feet. A small or storm jib or a large light-weather jib could be set to suit weather conditions and the work in hand, while a jib topsail and a balloon foresail could be carried in light weather, when a bowsprit spinnaker was often set to the topmast head, boomed out for running or sheeted in to serve as a balloon jib.

The jib sheets had no purchase and led in through holes in the bulwarks, then forward to make fast to the bitts, but the balloon foresail sheet was led aft, outside everything. The gaff averaged 25 feet in length and was hoisted by smack-style peak and throat halyards. The leech was almost parallel to the luff and the boomless foot of the sail very short. The luff was hooped to the mast and the main tack could be triced up with a tackle. A single brail was fitted, running from a block at the throat, around the leech and back again to another throat block and down to the deck. Both truss and brail were in constant use when working gear, to regulate speed without affecting the topsail, and two or three rows of reef points were also fitted. The mainsheet was arranged as already described and a bearing-out spar was used when running in light weather. The foresail (staysail) sheeted to a horse across the foredeck, and the fall of the halyard was always made fast to the neck of the lower block to retain it when it was lowered in haste.

The topsail was sometimes diagonally cut and the luff was laced, hooped or set on a jack-line to the topmast. In light weather the topsail often remained set above a brailed mainsail for ease of working, or if the bawley was anchored for a short time. In winter the bawleys often struck their topmasts and some removed them altogether. When the mainsail was lowered it was stowed along the gaff, with the peak on deck to one side.

With their small radius of forefoot and long straight keel a bawley kept its course well when sailing or hove to. The tiller had a pin rail to secure it, running across the after coaming, and this was known as the "old man" at Leigh as it freed the helmsman for work on deck in most conditions. With the foresail set just a'weather, these boats held their course for miles while the crew were culling, cooking and packing the catch. When hove to, most bawleys would fetch directly up to windward in any weather.

Originally all bawley sails were flax canvas, but later many had cotton sails. About 1910 a suit of sails for a bawley cost about £80, ordered by the owner direct from the sailmaker for a new boat. Usually these were made by F. A. Turnnidge of Leigh or Pennick of Harwich, both of whom specialised in the rig. A suit took about ten days to make. Francis Turnnidge made many of these for bawleys, besides a greater number of yacht sails and others for small sailing boats. Son of a bawley owner, he was apprenticed as a sailmaker at the sail loft at Leigh in 1894. The owner of the business died in 1900 and Francis was left to take over the business and run it until he retired in 1964 after 70 years in sailmaking.

A bawley took about six months to build, and construction was usually in the open. Over many years the majority of bawleys were built by Aldous at Brightlingsea, Essex, many being the creations of the yard foreman, Mr Foote, who produced shapely and well-built craft. The Aldous-built bawleys had more rounded sections than those of other builders and probably showed some smack influence. The bawley *Gladys* was built in 1898 by Aldous. Her dimensions were 36 feet overall length, 32 feet waterline length × 13 feet beam × 5 feet draught. J. and H. Cann of Harwich were noted builders of bawleys and their story will be told later. At Southend, Hayward, previously a boatbuilder at Deal in Kent, became a clever designer of bawleys and cockle boats, as well as sailing pleasure-boats and, later, motor craft. Hayward designed by draughting. Many fast sailers, particularly for owners at Southend, were launched from his yard near the gasworks, on the Eastern Esplanade.

Parsons of Leigh built the bawley *Enterprise*, among others. He had been apprenticed to Hayward and also built skiffs for bawleys and other small craft. His son followed him in the trade, building several fine motor shrimpers and cocklers, besides many small yachts. Bundock Brothers, also at Leigh, built several bawleys in their yard near the coastguard station, between the railway line and the sea wall. At the head of the creek several (modern) Leigh motor fishing boats were designed by Ernie Johnson of the boatbuilders Johnson Sons and Jago Ltd.

On the Medway, Gill of Rochester and E. Lemon of Strood built bawleys usually for owners in Kent, and Leigh fishermen seem frequently to have ordered bawleys from Aldous at Brightlingsea and the Canns at Harwich, and even from Peters at Southend, but the only instance I can discover of one being built on the Medway for Leigh was that built at Rochester by Gill for Fred Tomlin, which sailed well. Skifts for the bawleys were also built by King at Pin Mill, Suffolk, and by William King at Burnham.

As Leigh was not a port of registry the fishing vessels there bore the letters LO (London), HH (Harwich) or MN (Maldon), usually depending on where they were built or had originally been owned. Most craft built and originally owned at Leigh were registered LO with number.

The shrimp trawl used by a sailing bawley was typically about 21 feet long in the beam and had the usual iron trawl heads, with a bass rope bridle. This was attached to a large wooden bridle block through which the bass trawl warp was rove. The warp was made fast forward, to the windlass bitts at one end; the other was usually belayed amidships, perhaps to the wink post. The warp was pinned in to the rail to suit conditions of wind and tide and the direction in which the fisherman wished to tow the trawl. The shrimp net was of fine mesh, slacked back from its ground rope and well protected by chafing pieces on the underside of the cod end, which was of smaller mesh than the remainder of the net. When hoisted to dry a shrimp trawl presents a dense, dark curtain of mesh.

Shrimps have always been sold by capacity measure in gallons, pints or half pints. They were one shilling a gallon in 1900, when 86 bawleys sailed out of Leigh, which then also had 32 sailing cockle boats working. As late as 1930 there were still 72 sailing bawleys owned there.

A typical day's shrimping at Leigh before 1914 usually started early, probably in darkness, depending on the time of the tide. As the tide rose the fishermen walked across the mud towards their skifts, as the bawley's boats were called colloquially. Late arrivals clattered along the narrow High Street in nail-shod thigh boots, some picking up two or three wicker baskets, called pads, in which the shrimps were sent to market. They sculled off in the skift, a stoutly built clinker-planked boat about 14 feet long and usually painted a light blue. Skipper and mate pulled along, with an oar each, half a mile down the narrow creek to where the bawleys were anchored.

As they got on board there might be a southerly wind and both men worked at the windlass to get the anchor up and the sails hoisted. With all sails set the bawley, in company with several others, was carried with the light wind into the Low Way. Then it died, leaving the bawleys to anchor again against the strengthening flood tide to await a return of the breeze. The balloon foresail was hanked to the forestay and the spinnaker was substituted for the jib, but the calm persisted. However, the crew anticipated an easterly breeze which would strengthen in the afternoon to a true sea-breeze, only to die again at sunset, when the wind might swing northerly and then round through south by morning, a cycle known in Essex as "shrimpers' winds".

The mate lit the fo'c'sle stove and boiled the kettle for tea, and soon another breeze ruffled the water and the bawleys laboriously up-anchored again and cleared the point of Marsh End Sand, then drifted up the river, the strongly flooding Thames tide helping. Calms prevailed until high water, when the little fleet had reached Holehaven, at the north west side of Canvey Island. Meanwhile the crew had eaten breakfast. Some skippers tried to tow their trawls before the light breeze, but despite a boomed-out mainsail and spinnaker it was hopeless. However, as soon as the ebb tide started most of the bawleys prepared their trawls for shooting. First, the buoy, which was fastened to the cod end by a long rope as an alternative means of recovery of the trawl if it should "come fast", was thrown over the side. Then came the fine-meshed net by the armful, and finally the heavy trawl beam, with its iron heads, on which it sledged its way along the bottom with the net streaming from it like a great bag, was humped over the rail and the trawl warp was paid out. The average length of a trawl beam for a bawley of 32 to 35 feet was then 25 feet, but just before 1914 some Leigh boats were again working the old trim-tram type nets, four at a time.

As there was still little or no wind the bawleys drifted with the tide, broadside, with headsails lowered and the mainsail brailed up to steady the gaff as they rolled in the swells of passing steamers. These managed to avoid the dozen or so fishing boats. In darkness it was much more dangerous near the ship-channel and anywhere else when other sailing craft were about, such as barges, other fishing smacks and bawleys. Sometimes a sailing barge would have to let go her anchor to sheer clear of the gathering of trawling bawleys, leading to an exchange of views by all in earshot. After a while the skipper put his hand on the trawl warp, feeling how the net was moving by the vibrations travelling up the rope, which told him if all was well.

At intervals he dropped over the stern a tell-tale, a small shrimp-mesh net on a half-round iron, which had a hoeing edge, like a miniature trawl. It was allowed to drag for a short time and was hauled up for examination of a sample of what was to be caught below. Much of the time it was unfortunately only stones, weed and oddments—"dirt" to the fishermen.

Meanwhile, the mate was filling the copper in the hold with water from overside and then lighting the fire under it.

Off the Chapman Light the skipper decided to haul the trawl. The warp was passed around the wink and the mate and the skipper took the handles, the skipper also coiling the slack of the warp as best he could. Soon the bridle block came on board. Then the two hauled on the bridle until the fore end of the trawl appeared above water. The fish tackle was hooked to this and it was hoisted aboard. The after end was lifted on the rail and the trawl head was left hanging over the stern. Then the men heaved at the net until the heavy, bulging cod end appeared. The tackle was used to hoist this on deck. The cod and knot was untied and a wriggling mass of shrimps, crabs, seaweed and jelly fish shot out over the deck, perhaps with a few little flatfish or "dabs" struggling for life amongst the grey mass between bulwarks and hatch coaming.

By now a good breeze from the south-west might have arrived, and the jib was hoisted and sheets were gathered for a sail up again for the next haul. The skipper busied himself with the catch, scooping large handfuls into a circular sieve and at the same time quickly picking out weed and rubbish. He held it and shook the sieve while the mate washed the shrimps with buckets of water from overside. Washed and culled the selected shrimps were tipped into the now boiling copper. When the last of the catch was in the copper the net was shot again for a faster haul, as both wind and tide had strengthened.

About two bushels of brown shrimps were the result of the first haul, as the pink ones, which are the preferred type, could not be caught so far up. Suddenly there was a sharp crack, the warp ran quickly over the rail and the bawley was checked in the tideway. "She's fast", they shouted. Skipper and mate began the furious activity of hauling and then letting go of the warp, of bearing up to gather way and then suddenly luffing hard into the wind in attempts to free the net from whatever it had caught below. After considerable worrying of the trawl and a good deal of anxiety to the crew, for a ripped net could mean considerable loss in time and money, the skipper decided the trawl was free and the warp was hauled; perhaps the net was undamaged but turned inside out, with the consequent loss of the contents of the last haul. "Dropped in a hole made by the dredger and couldn't climb out properly", the skipper declared.

Still, sometimes it was worse, with the net foul of an old anchor or other sunken item, ripping the meshes and complicating repairs. However, a third haul brought a good catch, and still sieving and washing and boiling, with the trawl lying on the rail, the helm was put up for Leigh creek. The mate rigged a rectangular piece of net laced to two or more little poles laid between the lee rail and the hatch coamings. The shrimps were laid on this as they were ladled from the copper by a net with a handle to dry and be culled again for defective ones. Then they were shot into the pad baskets and sacking was stitched over the top, ready to be landed for the train when the bawley arrived.

The bawley rumbled along with a fair wind while the men worked; perhaps the helm was pegged with the "old man" rack at the after coaming. Then she was at the Low Way buoy and the helm was put down to surge up the channel, laying well to the now fresh south wester with a rumbling bow wave, then standing close-hauled up the Ray, between the double line of bawleys already anchored there. Foresail and jib were run down and the bawley shot up into her usual anchorage with twenty fathoms of cable following the anchor over the bows. It would be a further hour before the crew could get up the creek in the skiff, so they might turn to and stow the sails and gear in a leisurely manner, then have time for a nap before the water came, quickly as it does on that shallow, flat shore, and the pads were loaded into the skiff. The boat's mast and its lugsail were raised and with an oar over the stern they sailed and poled up the creek with the rising water until the boat grounded and they stepped overside to push her up to the Leigh, where the pads were carried quickly to the station to catch the train. This was a good day's work and typical of many I have spent shrimping from Leigh in motor shrimpers working the same waters in much the same way, with Arthur Cotgrove, Fred Hall or Ivan Emery in their smart little vessels. Some of the happiest days of my life have been in their company in Sea Reach or further seaward.

In earlier times and until the eighteen-fifties the Leigh fishermen had worked a fishery for cod and skate with long-lines, setting them anywhere between the Oaze Channel at the entrance of the Thames to Walton Naze or Orfordness to the north, depending on the season and movements of the fish. Whether this was carried on with bawleys or smacks is uncertain.

Wesley Bundock recalled talk at Leigh of bawleys sailing to the Channel

Islands in the mid-nineteenth century, possibly for smuggling but much more likely to dredge oysters. There was considerable oyster activity at Leigh until the end of the nineteenth century, with Alston's large smacks working from there, dredging in the North Sea and the English Channel. Because of the exposed nature of the approaches to Leigh Creek and the amount of bawley, cockle-boat and barge traffic in it, Alston's chose to lay their smacks up in the Swale when not in use. They also sometimes lay there awaiting orders. In Hadleigh Ray, oyster layings were at one time worked by Hobart and Hammond, who kept a watch smack there to guard the beds.

By 1872 shrimping had become the principal fishery of Leigh, employing between 70 and 80 vessels, the largest being transom-sterned bawleys, many then 32 feet overall length. When shrimps were scarce in the Thames and its approaches many Leigh fishermen sailed forty miles up the coast to Harwich, joining the fleet of smacks and bawleys working out of that north-east Essex port. They returned in September.

Sometimes in bad seasons Leigh craft worked on the south coast, using Shoreham in Sussex as a base. They also occasionally sailed to Holland, Belgium, France and the Channel Islands in search of shrimps to trawl or shellfish to dredge. A few Leigh bawleys worked out of Ostend, Belgium, for several seasons, and the bawley rig was adopted by some pointed-stern, cutter-rigged Belgium smacks which also shrimped from the port.

Like all fishing vessels, bawleys had their share of misfortune and in 1866 an insurance club was formed for Leigh fishing boats; sixty were entered that year. 1868 was a bad year for the Leighmen. There were no shrimps to be caught in the spring and no sprats in the late autumn and winter. As a result four boats were offered for sale and as things worsened there was great distress in Leigh, which lasted for some 18 months.

However, the insurance fund survived until at least the early eighteen-nineties, despite several severe shortages of shrimps and sprats. This was serious to a village where the population had no summer yachting or large-scale winter oyster fisheries to sustain them, as was so in the Colne and Blackwater rivers.

Although bawleys rarely had opportunity for salvage and did not seek it, they occasionally ventured out in hard weather. In March 1882 a sailing barge went ashore in the Jenkin Swatch, across the Thames from Leigh. The crew of two watched the Southend lifeboat battle across towards them as they lashed themselves in the barge's rigging. Then with horror they saw her turn back before the gale. The men were later rescued by the bawley *Seven Sisters*, sailed to their aid by Captain Wilder, one of Leigh's few yacht skippers, with Thomas Emery, a man named Lungley and two coastguards from Leigh as crew. This may have been the Wilder who at one time owned the bawley *Unity*.

The bawley *Violet* was built at Pin Mill, on the Suffolk river Orwell, in the eighteen-nineties. She was run down on her first trip and sank. Later she was raised and put ashore in Crowstone Bay, on the shore to the east of Leigh. Being run down by a ship in the Thames fairway or the estuary approaches was an ever-present fear when fishing at night or in fog, and besides the few that were run down there were many others that had close shaves. Steamers were not the only menace. Sailing barges and small sailing ships, such as the collier brigs and timber-carrying vessels from the Baltic, also took a toll and the bawleymen and cocklers took good care to see that their navigation lights were burning brightly.

As Southend grew and demand for fish and shrimps increased with its summer tripper trade, a fleet of about twenty bawleys became established there, lying on the hard and very exposed sandy foreshore. There was great rivalry between the fishermen of Southend and Leigh, the Leighmen regarding them as intruders in their long established fisheries. This feeling still existed in the motor fleets of both places in the nineteen-fifties.

Twenty to thirty bawleys from Leigh and Southend went stowboating for sprats before 1914, and there were more working the fishery in the mid and late nineteenth century.

Much of their catch was landed at Leigh at Bell Wharf, but a fair amount went to Strood and Chatham on the Medway or to Gravesend, for manure at about 30 shillings per ton, unloaded. The Leigh and Southend bawleys seem never to have landed catches at Brightlingsea, the centre of the sprat trade on the Essex coast.

The Leigh bawleys often launched their stowboat baulks and gear over the starboard side abaft the shrouds as the boat was anchored, when it had been given a hard sheer in a strong tideway. This was quicker than the usual method of working the baulks around and under the bow of a smack in order to stream the net, as was done by the Colne and Tollesbury smacks. This Leigh method was known as the flying shoot, as the gear had to be shot at speed and without a snag. If it went wrong a torn net resulted. Otherwise the Leigh and Southend stowboating seems to have followed the pattern of the Colne and Tollesbury smacks in gear and working.

However, bawleys from both places were for many years engaged in fishing for whitebait with a form of stow net. Two hands were enough to man a bawley when catching whitebait. Once the net was down they hove it up and recovered the catch from the cod end without bringing the beams and gear on deck, taking in the small quantities usually caught at a time and not needing the four-man crew of a stowboater after sprats, which might get a full net with several tons of fish to be handled quickly to avoid damage to smack and gear.

Whitebait consists principally of the small or fry of herring and sprats, with other species of fish besides. It has for centuries been a delicacy, served in London restaurants with more ceremony than even oysters, and a long-established Thames-side whitebait dinner was continued as a festival at Southend from the nineteen-thirties into the nineteen-seventies.

Greenwich and Gravesend fishermen were among the best-known seekers of whitebait. At first they used their little clinker-planked, pointed-sterned, rowing and sailing peter boats, which rode to anchor with miniature stow nets of fine mesh and a mouth only 3 to 4 feet square. The net was drawn in and emptied of its catch at intervals.

This river fishing was carried on upstream as far as Woolwich, though pollution was a problem even in the early nineteenth century. Soon it drove the Greenwich whitebait fishermen down river to Gravesend and to Leigh, along with their transom-sterned peter boats, which had been developed during the early nineteenth century. Leigh and Southend offered rail connections to London and the possibility of landing fish at Southend pier at any state of the tide. Moreover the estuary then had a wide choice of grounds to fish.

The whitebait fishermen were soon using bawleys of the usual Leigh or Harwich type and nets similar to the stow net used for sprats by the Colne and Tollesbury smacks. The nets had baulks about 25 feet long supporting a net of fine mesh which was short, often about 10 feet long; this needed frequent lifting to empty the catch. Whitebait fishing was principally an overnight or short period fishery, as the catch had to be landed as quickly as possible to be sent to market fresh on the train. The Young family of Greenwich were prominent in the whitebait fishery and moved downstream to Leigh at the end of the nineteenth century, when William Young and Son soon developed as fish merchants as well as fishermen. They took to shrimping and as their business grew acquired interests in the Grimsby fish trade, eventually becoming a large group of companies.

Other merchants were in the whitebait trade and Leigh became its centre at the turn of the century and later. In 1898 there were nine bawleys and sixteen open lugsail rowing and sailing boats, which were used after a change in fishery regulations of 1893 limited fishing above the Thames Conservancy (as it then was) limits. These were on a line between the Crowstone, on the Chalkwell shore, across to the Yantlet on the Kent side.

In that time the whitebait season lasted from February until August and was extended by the use of the small boats with seine nets, locally called drag nets.

The Leigh whitebait stowboaters had a crew of two and worked on a system of a share each and a third share for the bawley. If they also went drag-netting with a small boat, a third hand was shipped and the small boat was hired by the merchant for whom they were fishing, who also provided the net, boxes, and paid charges to get the catch to market. The grounds worked by the whitebait bawleys varied. Sometimes they fished in the Yantlet or upriver off Holehaven, at other times in the mouth of Hadleigh Ray, but usually a little group of them were anchored just below the end of Southend Pier where tidal streams meet and there was more chance of fish.

Like the spratters, the whitebait stowboaters watched for gulls feeding on the whitebait shoals or, to a lesser extent, for discoloration of the water in order to choose a place to anchor and shoot the net. Some thought the early flood was the best time for a good catch, others the ebb. It mattered little whether it was night or day.

Bawleys were still stowboating for whitebait in the mid-nineteen-fifties, when three or four from Leigh and Southend still anchored below Southend Pier in season, with nets streamed. It is believed that two of Young's bawleys continued into the mid-nineteen-sixties, but by then whitebait were being taken by modern motor-fishing boats using pair-trawl nets, the crews aided by echo sounders and fish-freezers to preserve the catch. The Gilson and Bridge families continued the trade in this form into the nineteen-seventies, landing from half a ton to one ton each day in good seasons.

Many whitebait crews fished in summer along the shore for whitebait with a seine net, in the same way that the Medway bawleymen captured smelts. The nets were about 40 fathoms long and 9 feet or so at the ends, increasing to about 15 feet in the centre, where a pocket was worked in about 15 feet long, having a cod end of finer mesh. The net was set by rowing out from the shore, where one man kept the end ropes, the others paying it out in a semi-circle to the shore, where two men drew it in while the third splashed the water with an oar to drive the fish into the pocket. Several hauls were made on each trip, and drag-netting was reckoned as laborious as stowboating for whitebait. The drag-netters worked along the shore from Southend, Shoebury and the Maplins' edge, and on the Kent side in the Swale and around the Isle of Sheppey.

A well-shaped clinker-planked boat about 17 feet long was developed for drag-netting. One of these could be towed by a bawley, which would remain anchored in deeper water while her crew rowed inshore to set the drag net. Sometimes these whitebait boats were used as the sole craft to carry the net and three men, either under oars or sometimes with a lugsail or a lug and foresail rigged set on a mast, which could be quickly struck for rowing.

The shapely whitebait boats attracted the attention of local sailing men and in 1904 the Essex Yacht Club, with headquarters at Leigh in the hulk *Gipsy*, established a 17 foot Whitebait Restricted Class. The purpose was to provide inexpensively-built boats for pleasure use in racing and day-sailing. When their racing days were over these were to be sold for use by local whitebait fishermen. Fifteen boats were built to the class in seven years by Bundock Brothers of Leigh, J. and H. Cann of Harwich, Hayward of Southend, Peters of Southend, Aldous of Brightlingsea, Forrestt and Co. of Wivenhoe, and the Burnham Yacht Building Company, which produced the sleekest design of all within the strict rule requirements, built by that consummate small-boat designer Harry Smith. There is no record that any of these boats were afterwards used for fishing, but they certainly provided good racing.

The bawleys and peter boats also worked peter nets or stop nets for flatfish, the bawleymen using their "skift" or small boat to set and recover the nets and seines, which were also used for smelts and whitebait. They also went hoop-netting for dabs, working several nets from the bawley and one or two from the boat lying astern.

Southend grew popular with day trippers after the mid-nineteenth century and thousands arrived there by train from London at weekends and holidays into the nineteen-sixties. They created a demand for sailing trips off the beach and many passenger sailing boats were built, usually rigged bawley fashion, sometimes with a mizzen added. The smaller ones generally resembled the sailing cockle boats but a few larger ones, such as the *Volunteer*, were open boats of bawley size and proportions, usually having a foredeck and a short afterdeck. The large amidships well had thwarts for the passengers. Many had a centreplate after about 1900. Several were built by Hayward, after he opened his yard at Southchurch, Southend, in the 1880s, after moving there from Deal in Kent. The *Skylark* of 1886 was followed a year later by *Jubilee*, built for George and Alfred Myall of the well known local fishing family. The *May Queen*, *Storm King*, *Four Brothers* and *Moss Rose* followed and then the largest of the sailing pleasure boats, the *Victoria* and *Prince of Wales*.

The larger boats were rigged as gaff ketches or dandies, the smaller usually as sloops, which were sometimes worked by one man, quite a handful with probably twenty or more people on board. The larger boats carried perhaps sixty or so, and at a shilling each this represented a sound income when a man's wage was no more than thirty shillings per week.

In later years Peters at Leigh also built pleasure sailing boats including the 27 foot *Coronation* and *Princess* and the little sloop-rigged *Irene*, which managed to load up to twenty-two trippers. Others were built at Brightlingsea by Aldous and all had a regular pitch on the crowded beaches of summer, where there was rivalry between boatmen working the east beach and those the west beach. The pier was the dividing line, jutting into the Thames about one and a quarter miles, carrying an electric railway and thousands more trippers, besides acting as a lifeboat station and landing place for fish, pilots, yachtsmen and others. Each pitch had a wooden wheeled stage, which was run out so that the shallow-hulled pleasure boat could get her quarter alongside and the trippers could then board without getting wet. Occasionally smaller bawleys or cockle boats were also used for tripping, but their decks and general arrangements were unsuitable for tripping with large numbers.

In winter some of the larger sailing pleasure boats went stowboating for sprats, though the open well made the crew sail with caution. A loose false deck of boards was laid over the thwarts in the well for the crew to work on and the catch was shot out below this, after which they had to be sailed even more carefully, as sprats are a cargo which is very liable to shift suddenly. Motorboats began to challenge the sailing pleasure boats before 1914 and after 1918 steadily ousted them, though several smaller sailing boats worked into the nineteen-fifties and the last, the *Irene*, gave up in 1971.

There were races for bawleys at both Leigh and Southend regattas. Leigh regatta was reckoned the premier event, and at both they raced for a championship flag and a money prize. Entries seem to have been only local and bawleys from the Medway and Harwich did not compete. The Leigh regattas just before 1914 were the heyday of the bawleymen. A committee barge was moored off the Bell Wharf and music was supplied by C. F. D. Bundock's band, who had their refreshments supplied, as did the committeemen on the barge. Much of the credit for these events was due to Francis Turnnidge, the Leigh sailmaker, who acted as the secretary. The 1910 regatta cost £104 3s 3d to hold, subscribed locally, of which £56 15s 0d was disbursed in prize money. The winning bawley and cockle boat each received a championship flag for its respective class, presented by Mr Turnnidge. There were also rowing, sculling and swimming races, climbing the greasy pole and fireworks in the evening.

The 1912 bawley race was typical. Competitors were allowed half a minute per foot overall as handicap. The prizes were £4 and a championship flag for the first, £3 second and £1 for the third and fourth bawley, to encourage a good entry. That year they started at 1.15 pm on a course with the start marked between a boat and two flags in Crowstone bay, continuing round the Low Way buoy, and finishing between a Union Jack mark and the committee barge, leaving all marks to starboard.

The prizewinners were the *Vera*, A. Kirby (built by Aldous), *Nil Desperandum*, W. Oliver, *Doris*, W. Lucking and *Honor*, F. C. Cotgrove. The *Doris* won. The 41 foot 6 inches long *Doris* was built by J. and H. Cann in 1910 and was named for the owner's daughter. She won the Leigh bawley races in 1910, 1911, 1912 and 1913. There were of course no races during the 1914–18 war; as Mr Lucking continued to use his sails throughout it, by its end they were well worn. He could not then afford new sails of racing cut, and the speedy *Doris* was never again to appear as champion bawley at Leigh and the *Helen and Violet* took the honour, partially, it was said, because Mr Felton had a relative in the sailmaking business at Southampton, a source from which he was able to obtain new sails. However, the *Doris* was a very fast boat, cleverly sailed. A few years ago she was restored to sailing condition.

The 1912 Leigh regatta also offered races for yachts (boats) under 17 feet long. There were six entries. Another race was for yachts under 25 feet, with seventeen entries, and one for yachts over 25 feet, which attracted nine entries. Four motor boats started in a handicap race, followed by the Essex Yacht Club 17 foot One-Design Class. There was a veterans' sculling race for over sixty-fives, with a first prize of a new guernsey and 2s 6d, second prize a guernsey, third half a ton of coal and fourth a quarter of a ton of coal.

In 1913 this race attracted five starters, the oldest aged seventy-seven. There was a Millers versus Sweeps event—a variant of the Colne and Blackwater pull Devil–pull Baker, with two men in two bawley's boats made fast by a length of rope from each transom, pelting each other with paper bags of soot and chalk. A race peculiar to Leigh was one in which fishermen in thighboots competed on the foreshore. Climbing the greasy pole at Leigh was done vertically and ashore—a much more difficult feat than walking the usually hazardous horizontal one, rigged out from a committee boat's side over the water, with a flag at its end as a prize for those skilful enough to stay on. At Leigh the prize was sometimes a live piglet.

Alfred Kirby of Leigh enjoyed racing a bawley and was one of the few Leigh men who participated in yacht racing. For several years before 1914 he acted as local pilot in the races from the lower Thames of the big class yachts. He was often on board the royal racing cutter *Britannia*, giving the benefit of his extensive local knowledge of tidal sets, depths and local wind shifts to her captain, at first John Carter and later his son "Jack" Carter, of Rowhedge. Alf Kirby owned the bawleys *Fiona* and *Marion*. The 40 foot × 13 foot 8 inches *Fiona* was built at Harwich by J. and H. Cann. The 36 foot *Marion* was by Peters of Southend and was not too well formed and an indifferent sailer. Mr Kirby was at Harwich when Bill Lucking's bawley *Doris* was on the stocks in 1910 and pointed her out to his young son as a very promising entry for the next year's Leigh regatta. Other Kirbys owned the bawleys *Ena*, *Florence*, *Alice* and the *Bona*, named after the large racing cutter of the late eighteen-nineties, which was also probably piloted in the Thames matches by a Kirby, possibly Alfred.

After the difficult but relatively prosperous fishing years of the 1914–18 war and its immediate aftermath, when sea-food was in demand, it became increasingly harder to make a living under sail, and the price of shrimps in the nineteen-twenties fell slightly to 10 pence per gallon, with a deduction at Leigh for landing dues. Some owners at Leigh had engines fitted, many of them 18 hp Kelvin petrol-paraffin models, others 7–9 hp Thornycroft Handybillies. Sails began to be discarded and the mainmast of some bawleys was shortened, though almost all retained the topsail and jib bowsprit.

Despite these changes Leigh Regatta still held a bawley race at intervals. The Young family entered their bawley *Alice Matilda* and later the smaller bawley *Prima Donna*. Their crews were given £1 as compensation for the lost day's fishing and about £50 was spent on preparing the bawley, the bottom being blackleaded to achieve a high finish. Yard topsails and spinnakers were at that period borrowed from local yachts and account for the amazing sail spreads shown in contemporary photographs. A barge was moored off Bell Wharf at Leigh as committee boat for the regatta.

Two bawleys kept their sailing gear in full rig: Arthur Felton's *Helen and Violet* and Sidney Cotgrove's *Olive*, then recently brought to Leigh and usually sailed when racing by Alf Kirby. In the last race for sailing bawleys at Leigh

Regatta in 1928 these two rivals started in a squally north-west wind and had just rounded the Chapman Head lighthouse, with the *Olive* leading by about 250 yards, when a squall caught the *Helen and Violet* and laid her on her beam ends. Water started to run below and her keel was visible, but she slowly recovered. Arthur Cotgrove, who sailed in her that day, told me they all thought she would capsize. The *Olive* was later sold to an owner in Southend and ended by breaking adrift from her moorings on the foreshore and being pounded to pieces against Southend Pier, as the bawley *Nil Desperandum* had been in 1914, when her crew of three were drowned.

It is believed that the *Saxonia* was the last bawley built. She was constructed by Aldous Successors Ltd at Brightlingsea for W. Young and Son of Leigh. She was not a true sailing bawley, although now she is rigged as such, but had an engine installed when built. She may also have been the last bawley built there under Mr Foote, the foreman, who had supervised the building of many.

Aldous' quotation for building the *Saxonia* was £510. A separate price for the supply of the mainsail, staysail and jib in best flax canvas was £110. Constructed of the best materials for a fishing boat she was a loss to the yard, a not uncommon result when building wooden vessels. The *Saxonia* was built for Youngs and was to be worked from Burnham on Crouch, under a skipper named Surs. She is now rigged and sails for pleasure, a use for bawleys which would puzzle their original owners.

In 1934 there were twenty-two bawleys still working from Leigh; four years later there were only fourteen. The others were sold to yachtsmen for conversion for pleasure sailing, £110 being a typical price, or were broken up for firewood. Some were left in marsh rills to decay, for as the older man died or gave up fishing, younger crews could not be found for them. They were attracted into the new motor shrimpers and cocklers, which could earn more with fewer demands on the crew.

A few bawleys lingered on under power into the early nineteen-fifties, used for whitebait fishing. I recall seeing two or three at work with their stow nets at that time, usually seaward of Southend Pier. The *Saxonia* was among these last before she was sold for conversion to an oyster dredger on the Colne fishery, where she worked through the nineteen-sixties and -seventies. In 1979 she was re-rigged to be used for pleasure sailing.

A similar happy ending came to the little *Prima Donna*, owned latterly by William Woodward of Wivenhoe. That good fisherman worked her under power during the nineteen-thirties and into the nineteen-fifties, when in 1954 I designed a new motor shrimper for his principal trade. The *Laura* was the last wooden fishing vessel built at the Rowhedge yards and embodied my experience and observation during the many holiday days spent shrimping with the Leighmen, under power. The *Prima Donna* was re-rigged as a cutter yacht sailing from the Newtown River in the Solent, where Bill Woodward had raced often.

Fig. 26. The Leigh bawley *Helen and Violet* after racing at Leigh regatta in 1922. This photograph gives a good impression of the bawley's power to carry sail in smooth water. This quarter view of her beamy hull, with her augmented regatta-day crew standing nonchalantly about the deck, emphasises her initial stability. The *Helen and Violet* (remembered at Leigh as the *Ellen and Violet*) was built at Harwich by J. and H. Cann in 1906 and in the nineteen-twenties was the fastest of the remaining sailing bawleys at Leigh, the *Doris* having retired from racing. She won the bawley race at Leigh in 1921, 1922 and 1923 in the ownership of Arthur Felton. The large topsail carried here has an unusually long topsail yard to keep the luff straight. The jackyard, extending the clew, is bending in the way such spars often do, but the topsail sets flat except at the tack. She is standing in for the shore off Chalkwell, then still largely unblemished by house-building. A fine picture of a smart fishing boat, still sailing as a yacht from Brightlingsea.

Fig. 27. The Leigh bawley *Doris* shrimp-trawling in light airs in the lower Thames. Her mainsail (trysail) has one reef taken in the foot and a jib-headed topsail is set above. The balloon jib or "bowsprit spinnaker" is set in place of the working jib, which lies along the bowsprit. The staysail (foresail) is run down the forestay. Her crew of two, Mr William Lucking, the owner, and his mate, are busy sieving the catch of shrimp on deck, picking out the best and shooting them into the boiling copper, the smoke from which is blowing away from the chimney.

For several years before 1914 the *Doris* was the fastest bawley. She was built in 1910 by J. and H. Cann of Harwich and was always well sailed and successful in the fisheries.

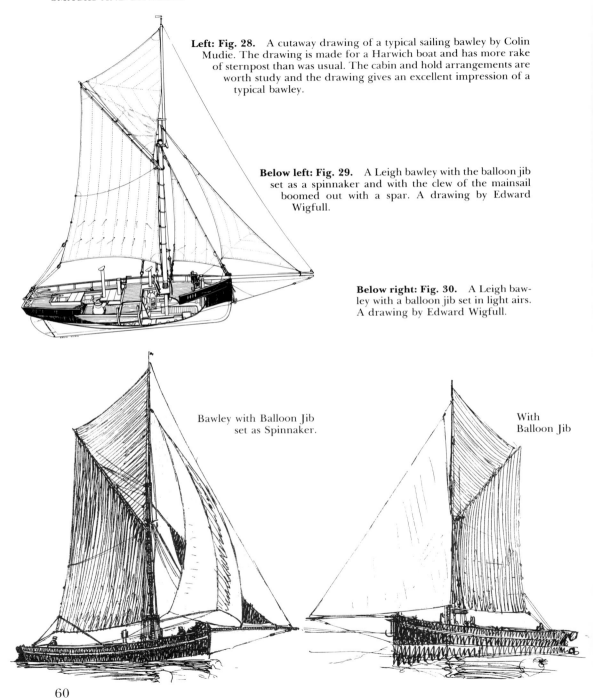

Left: Fig. 28. A cutaway drawing of a typical sailing bawley by Colin Mudie. The drawing is made for a Harwich boat and has more rake of sternpost than was usual. The cabin and hold arrangements are worth study and the drawing gives an excellent impression of a typical bawley.

Below left: Fig. 29. A Leigh bawley with the balloon jib set as a spinnaker and with the clew of the mainsail boomed out with a spar. A drawing by Edward Wigfull.

Below right: Fig. 30. A Leigh bawley with a balloon jib set in light airs. A drawing by Edward Wigfull.

Bawley with Balloon Jib set as Spinnaker.

With Balloon Jib

60

Fig. 31.   The Leigh bawley 195 LO at anchor with jib and foresail run down and the mainsail triced up at the luff, the topsail remaining set above. The trawl beam is on deck but does not appear to have a net bent to it. This photograph shows some detail of the standing and running rigging of a sailing bawley and her lofty rig. The lightboards are in place on the shrouds, ready for the lamps to be shipped. These craft needed efficient lights, as they worked in the entrance to the River Thames, which then carried large numbers of ships large and small, at all hours. A photo taken in the nineteen-twenties.

Above: Fig. 32. Leigh bawley with engine under reduced rig in the nineteen-thirties. Topmasts and crosstrees have been laid ashore but the three lower sails remain in use to conserve fuel and as a precaution against engine breakdown. The white painting of the lower transom was common at Leigh and provided some help in seeing the craft ahead in fog or at night, particuarly in the narrow creek and its approaches.

Above: Fig. 34. View of the Leigh bawley LO 384 dried out off Leigh. This shows the well-formed hull of many bawleys and the length of the topmast. The entrance of the hull is fine and the run hollow and shapely. The joining connectors in the topmast shrouds allowed the lower parts to be disconnected when the topmast was housed to reduce windage and top-hamper in bad weather.

Opposite page, bottom: Fig. 33. 195 LO in a light breeze and probably aground, waiting to sail off, as indicated by her skiff, under her lee side, although her sails are drawing. The photograph is interesting as it shows the foot of the mainsail "picked up" with reef points to reduce area and help control speed for trawling; as a consequence, the gaff is not hoisted up the mast as high as when the full mainsail was set, and the topsail is also slacked down to suit. The small jib is set part-way along the bowsprit on its traveller to balance the sails set. The skipper stands aft waiting for her to float.

63

Above: Fig. 35. A 17 foot whitebait boat of the type developed to work a drag or draw seine net along the shore with two or three men. These were fine, seaworthy boats which were often towed astern of a bawley to the location of their work. Most could also be sailed under a lugsail, and it is believed that some later boats were built with a centreplate. The mast and sail are lying in the boat. The fisherman is rowing standing facing forward and pushing on the oars, a much used method known as "sheaving". It is useful in smooth water but more difficult and less efficient in rough. A photograph taken about 1921.

Left: Fig. 36. The bawley *Saxonia* was the last to be built, by Aldous Successors Ltd at Brightlingsea in 1928, for William Young and Son Ltd at Leigh. Although her hull form, scantlings and arrangements were in the manner of her many predecessors under sail, the *Saxonia* was built to be worked under power in her owner's principal trade, stowboating for whitebait, though she was also sometimes used for fish-trawling. After many years' fishing from Leigh and from the river Crouch, she was bought by the Colchester Oyster Fishery Co., subsequent to its reconstruction after the disastrously cold winter of 1962 which almost wiped out the stocks of the Colne oysters. She became one of two vessels dredging the fishery with two dredges operated by a winch in place of the centuries-old method of hand-dredging. After several years in this work the *Saxonia* was converted to a rigged bawley in 1979. Here she sails in light airs during the 1979 Colne smack and barge race. The rig follows bawley practice. Many sailing bawleys were built by Aldous and she is the most modern afloat.

Fig. 37. Heaving up stowboat gear with the handspike windlass of a Leigh bawley fishing for whitebait in the estuary of the Thames.

Fig. 38. Opening the cod end of the stowboat net on deck.

Fig. 39. Spirited bawleys racing in a Leigh regatta. The bawley third from right carries a flag low down on her topmast forestay, a custom in many local regattas and also common in sailing barge races of the time.

CHAPTER FIVE

The Cocklers of Leigh

THE centre of cockling at Leigh has for long been situated in a series of black weatherboard sheds lining the creek side of the track which leads west beyond the High Street of the old village of Leigh. A few of its old cottages remain, mingled with more modern buildings. It is backed on the landward side by the railway line to London, an important link for the bygone fishing industry of Leigh after its arrival in 1854. Each cockle shed has a stovepipe and, facing the track, a square opening before which, in summer, a wide let-down flap or a trestle table covered with a white cloth, bears a tempting array of small saucers heaped with a pyramid of cockles. Bottles of vinegar, salt and pepper jostle with shellfish of other kinds, which find a ready sale to visitors and locals.

These cockle sheds have been the base of operations for the Leigh cockle industry for several generations of the various families that follow the trade; Osborne, Harvey, Dench, Meddle and Noakes were and are some of their names. Inside the sheds the cockles are cooked by steam, which also kills any bacteria. A huge heap of fresh-landed cockles occupied a corner of each cement-floored shed, where water always seemed to be running. The heaps were constantly being replenished by fresh landings by the cockle boat belonging to the "firm". A worker filled a perforated steel tray with cockles and opened the lid of the steamer to thrust it in, slamming the door and turning an hourglass nearby to time the cooking. From another steamer he took another tray which had been cooked for the stipulated time, its cockles steaming, shells gaping. These were poured into a rectangular sieve that hung from the roof above a large steel tank full of clean water. He riddled the cockles and shells quickly, the cockle meat falling through the sieve into the tank. The still-steaming empty shells he tossed through an open window with a deft flick of the sieve, to fall on the already gigantic mound below, ready to be carted away for making up paths, to be ground into chicken grit or spread along the foreshore to make up the landings for more cockle catches, or for use as foundations for oyster layings.

The cockles were transferred from the tank with a sort of landing net having a short handle and a stirrup-shaped iron frame. From the tank they went into a tub of clean water to wash out any sand or grit. Finally, if the cockles were to be kept for a day or so they were placed in a tub of clean brine.

Originally the cocklers laid their catches in Leigh Creek so that the cockles could purge themselves of impurities for a few days before they were taken to the sheds to be boiled in coppers of hot water. In the eighteen-nineties there was a major poisoning scare at Leigh caused by the alleged contamination of the cockle and nearby oyster beds by sewage discharge. This caused a temporary closure of the cockle beds and the oyster and winkle merchants close by. Eventually the practice of temporarily laying the cockles in Leigh Creek was forbidden and cooking by steam was stipulated by the health authorities.

Cockling at Leigh was carried on all year round. The cockle boats sailed to various grounds with a crew of three or four. They worked on the Main, as the flats along the Essex coast between Bradwell's Sales Point at the mouth of the river Blackwater and the mouth of the river Crouch were known, usually taking two tides to get there, going through the Havengore creeks or alternatively sailing around the Maplin sand and the Whittaker. The Maplin and Shoebury sands were favourite grounds, and on the Kent shore they worked off Seasalter, on the Pollard, the Leysdown Flats and at times in the area of the Jenkin Swatchway, the Yantlet Flats and the Grain Spit at the mouth of the Medway. They might take two tides to reach the Pollard grounds, rowing there in calms and keeping a good lookout for the wash of the mail steamer into Queen-borough, which the cocklers called Flashy Jack because of her speed.

Unfortunately many of the beds on the Maplin and Shoebury sands were found on the flats used by the artillery range and so these could be worked only when firing was not taking place. Before the use of telephones, two or three of the cocklers had to go down to the barracks at Shoebury on a Monday morning to get the firing orders for the week, so that they could plan their work.

A typical day's cockling under sail was for the boats to leave their moorings off each cockle shed at about 7.30 am if high water was at 8.30 am, with perhaps a light southerly wind. If firing was taking place on the Maplins the little fleet of a dozen or so cocklers stood across the mouth of the Thames towards the Grain Sand on the Kentish shore, above the entrance to the River Medway. The boats were soon strung out according to their sailing qualities. In summer they would be under mainsail, foresail, jib and perhaps with the topsail set. In winter the topmast was often housed. By the time they reached the river Middle buoy the weather might well have changed, with darker clouds and a rising wind, to which the light cocklers heeled, headed so that they had to make a tack or two to clear the Jenkin buoy. Then they could stand in over the sands until close to the shore of the low, flat Isle of Grain.

When the skipper judged they were over a suitable place one of the crew thrust a long sweep overboard and jabbed downwards to feel the sand surface for a thickly cockle-strewn space. When he and the skipper were satisfied, the anchor was let go and the sails lowered and stowed. Other cocklers would also be selecting their stations, and some, uncertain of the ground, could well move anchorage once or twice. The crew had to wait for the tide to ebb and went below to cook fried food for dinner or eat their sandwiches. There was little headroom in the fo'c'sle of a cockler and they sprawled on the wide locker-top bunks.

Forward was the cable locker and spare sails and gear encumbered the limited space, which also had the heel of the mast and a coal stove at its after end. Eating, yarning and sometimes playing cards the crews whiled away the time until the tide fell and the cocklers could take the ground as the water ebbed away.

With the sand dry, the crew went over the side, placing a couple of boxes or a plank on two trestles to form a platform of convenient height on which to step and tip the cockles into the hold. Each man had two baskets of about bushel size which, when full, could be carried by a wooden yoke across his shoulders. This yoke had a short rope at each end, ending in a hook to slip under the basket handles. It is not clear when yokes were first used. Earlier the baskets were carried individually. Each cockler had two short-handled rakes. One, like an ordinary garden rake, was used to dig into the muddy sand, raking the cockles which lay just beneath the surface in a series of sweeping arcs, bringing them into a sandy heap, almost between his feet. Then, changing to the other rake, the picker-up, which had a wooden bar and teeth of strong wire, he scooped the cockles into a net bag, the mouth of which was spread by a stirrup-shaped iron with a short wooden handle. This was usually rested against the left leg of the worker during the preliminary raking. When the bag was full the cockles were rinsed in the water of one of the many shallow pools left on the sands and were then tipped into the baskets. When these were full they were carried to the boat and were tipped into the hold.

Sometimes the cockles lay thick in the sands and the crew need go no further than perhaps fifty yards from the boat. At others, they were scattered and the heavy baskets had to be carried some distance and took longer to fill. It was hard work and particularly trying on the back and arms, but large quantities were gathered in this way during the course of one low water, sometimes in two. The men would straighten up for a few moments at times and rest, looking at the ever-changing panorama of traffic in and out of the river Thames, from liners to sailing barges, in those days of the Empire and of vigorous trade.

The rising tide, coming quickly at last over the flat sands, stopped the work when perhaps two tons of cockles had been gathered and shot into the hold. This cargo was spread evenly to trim the boat, and after putting a tripping line on the anchor, to ensure its quick recovery, the crew again went below to tea, possibly with a rising wind quickening the flames of the stove. With sufficient water the cocklers got under way, the crews hauling the anchors home quickly, perhaps with a reef or two in the mainsails. After dark, the sidelights were lit and shipped, as the boat would cross the shipping lane in the river on the passage home.

The cockle boats were naturally stiffer with a load of cockles on board and went plunging and sheering across the tideway towards the Essex shore, keeping a particular lookout for sailing barges and bawleys setting out for their night's work, as their sidelights were sometimes obscured by sails. About thirty minutes' sailing brought the cocklers to the leading lights for the Low Way. They stood close hauled up the narrow channel, with other boats close ahead and astern, rushing along in the darkness in between the steep banks of the narrow and winding Leigh Creek as it filled, and then across the surrounding flats covered by only two feet or so of water as the tide rose. The foresail might be lowered in these conditions, but their speed was still considerable in a reaching wind. If the boat went aground, as it might, then with shouts and hails several others would shoot head to wind to avoid a collision, some perhaps to get ashore temporarily, then off again, pushing desperately with sweeps in the gurgling tide. Then "Up peak" and "In with the jib" and they were off again up the creek to shouts of "Luff-up" or "Bear-up" from those ahead and astern, smelling the weather mud. Finally they threaded their way through the tangle of anchored bawley skiffs and up past the dark quays with the moored barges, to pick up the moorings off the cockle sheds and leave the unloading of the catch until next morning.

The Leigh "cockle galley" developed as a type with a rig identical to that of the bawley. Cocklers were shoal-draught boats which had a strong bottom to stand frequent grounding on the sands of the Thames estuary. Cocklers worked all year round and had at times to face rough weather on passage. They had also to be fast to sail to the grounds before the water left and to sail home as quickly as possible, when necessary with a heavy load of several tons of cockles. They had also to be capable of sailing well when loaded or light, as ballast was not carried. Until about 1900, old warship's boats about 25 to 28 feet long were reputedly converted for this work, bought cheaply from the dockyards at Sheerness and Chatham. The term "cockle galleys" is supposed to derive from this. These boats were "rose on" by 15 inches or so each side and were then decked over, leaving a narrow bawley-style hatch and providing a small cuddy forward for the crew. A boomless mainsail and foresail rig, sometimes also with a bowsprit and jib, was fitted. The hull planking was often doubled to strengthen the bottom and some had a false keel of wood bolted on to improve sailing qualities. A few had a centreplate installed. One of the ex-Naval galleys was named *Pretoria*, which dates her conversion. Sixty baskets of cockles filled one of these old-style cocklers, each basket holding six gallons, and it might take two or three tides to make this "catch", depending on the grounds.

Records show that two brothers Cundy owned two ex-ship's lifeboats which they rigged and used for cockling, usually selling their catch to other cocklers. Leigh cockling continued to be carried on with nondescript boats until about 1901, when several Leigh men sought larger and better craft. That year "Franny" Noakes had the carvel planked *Lily and Ada* built by Hayward of Southend. Like all her successors under sail she was arranged with a fo'c'sle with low headroom and locker berths on each side, a stove, and a bulkhead from the hold amidships which was divided from the steering room aft by another transverse bulkhead. The hold was ceiled for the catch. A long bawley-style hatch allowed wide side decks and the rig was a boomless-mainsail cutter of bawley style and proportions, but of course less area because of her smaller size. She was followed by the *Baden Powell* (Mr Osborne), *Shah, Jane Helen* ("Toodley" Meddle), and *Florence Edith* (Mr Axcell). These established a new type of cockler. Typical dimensions were 28 feet by 9 feet by 2 feet 6 inches draught of hull, with length increasing later to 32 to 33 feet, with beam in proportion. Most had a steel centreplate of considerable size, the case of which divided the hold and so formed a shifting bulkhead for the cargo. Some were built without a centreboard and had a deeper wooden keel, shaped up at the ends, to aid windward sailing. All were fairly flat bottomed to take the ground readily and were strongly built to withstand carrying several tons of cockles when aground and also to resist pounding when settling or, more usually, when leaving the sands. The transom stern had a slight rake and the rig was the same as a bawley, which at a distance these boats greatly resembled, except that they did not have a handspike windlass; so the anchor and cable was recovered by hand, readily done with their usual crew of three or four.

The nature of the work enabled the cocklers to be smartly kept, and early in this century many had the bottom blackleaded to achieve best speed when sailing to and from the grounds. There were eventually about 15 of these cocklers including the *Rover* (Joe Hills), *Three Brothers* (owned by three brothers Frost), *Liberty* (owned by a Mr Turnnidge) *Unknown* (Joe Deal) and *Gilbert* (owned by Richard Harvey, who later had the *Shamrock* built). The *Jessie Rebecca* was one of the smaller at 28 feet length and was built without a centreboard, but her finer bottom shape and false keel gave some windward ability. This type could not sail to windward as well as the centreplate boats but when loaded and with the wind free were equally fast.

A man named Barr built one cockle boat on the wharf in front of the *Crooked Billet* public house. S. J. Peters of Southend built the *Alice and Florrie* in 1905, a centreplate cockler 30 feet by 10 feet by 3 feet 3 inches hull draught. She sailed well and was sold for conversion to a yacht in 1935. Her centreplate was removed but despite this she could sail to windward in the river Blackwater at the same speed as a Maldon smack of similar size.

Size increased until about 1912, when Hayward built two 34-footers. The sail areas of one, the *Shamrock*, were mainsail, 416 square feet, topsail 168 square feet, foresail (staysail) 83 square feet, working jib 86 square feet; total 753 square feet. A balloon jib and a spinnaker were also carried and a storm jib could be set in strong winds. The *Shamrock* was the first cockler to have a well-rounded stem profile and like most of her contemporaries was designed by Hayward, who was a talented draughtsman and laid his craft off for fairing before commencing construction. His yard was near the Southend gasworks, on the Eastern Esplanade, not far from the rival boatyard of Peters. Hayward's office walls were lined with half models of his craft. He was a good businessman, originating from

Deal in Kent, where he had built beach boats. He established at Southend in 1885. His larger boats built there, including sailing and motor pleasure-tripping craft of up to 40 to 50 feet in length, were launched on a large, wheeled cradle towed by a steam traction engine. He was building motor pleasure boats and other craft into the mid-nineteen-twenties. The owners were very proud of the new breed of sailing cocklers and sailed them well, necessary when bound light for the cockle grounds as no ballast, except for a little trimming, was carried on the light draught. They raced as a class at Leigh regatta.

The 33 foot sister ships *Reindeer* and *Mary Amelia* were the last sailing cocklers built by Hayward, launched in 1914 for owners in Leigh. The last centreboard sailing cockler from Leigh was owned by "Choot" Johnson (how fishermen love nicknames). She was built by J. and H. Cann at Harwich and was a smart sailer into the nineteen-twenties, when most of the cockle boats had motors installed, though they continued to sport the full rig. During the 1914–18 War several cockle boats had 7–9 hp auxiliary engines installed, encouraged by the rapid acceptance of motor propulsion ashore and afloat. After the war new cocklers were built which were fifty-fifty craft, with rigs, until by 1928 full powered motor cocklers were being built, though these too retained a pole-masted cutter rig, with a bowsprit but without a topmast, topsail, balloon jib or spinnaker. By 1928 Leigh regatta was providing a race for cockle boats with auxiliary engines, offering prizes commensurate with those for the bawley races. The *Reindeer* (A. Noakes), *Resolute* (C and W. Osborne), *Kastoria* (J. Livermore) and *Victory* (W. Going) and *Ethel* (A. Noakes) started, with *Ethel* the winner.

The size of these cocklers increased, and two of the type built at Leigh by Cole and Wiggins, probably to the design of Harry Smith of Burnham on Crouch, were amongst the finest before 1939. The *Reliance* was 40 feet overall length by 12 feet beam and drew 2 feet. She had the usual transom stern and retained the large centreplate and the pole-masted auxiliary rig. Her fo'c'sle was 14 feet 6 inches long and was raised one strake above the sheer line to give 4 feet 8 inches headroom below. The hold was 14 feet 6 inches long, followed by an engine space 8 feet long and beyond that the after deck. She carried a bawley mainsail, a foresail and a jib set on a short bowsprit. Carvel planked on sawn oak frames, she was strongly built for almost continuous use, as these motor cocklers could carry a larger crew, perhaps six men, and could bring back a greater load than earlier boats. A 30 hp Kelvin petrol-paraffin motor was installed in the *Reliance*, but like her motor contemporaries she still set all possible sail during the runs to and from the grounds. By the late nineteen-twenties there were about 15 cockle boats at Leigh; these worked five and sometimes six days each week, all year round.

The Leigh cockle boats continued to develop as motor-sailers during the nineteen-thirties. Two of the type, the *Renown* and *Letitia*, sailed from Leigh to assist in the evacuation from Dunkirk in 1940. They rescued many from the beaches as their shoal draught enabled them to go close inshore, and they made several trips. Returning empty on 1st June, the *Renown* struck a mine and was blown up with all hands: skipper William Noakes, Frank and Leslie Osborne, all of Leigh, and naval rating Harold Porter.

The Leigh cockle boats further developed into fully powered craft after 1945, when several fine new ones were built, including a new *Renown*. I spent many happy hours on board them in the summers of 1948 to 1953, sharing the cocklers' life for pleasure during my holidays. Much of this was in the 40 foot *Navigator*, owned by Bert Osborne, and also aboard the last motor cockler built with a sailing rig, the splendid *Theodore E.M.* owned by the Meddle family and built at Maldon, Essex, by Dan Webb in 1947. She is now a yacht on the river Deben, as is the last *Renown*.

Survivors of this fleet still work from Leigh, but since 1967 hand raking has been replaced by mechanical dredging, working over the side of the boat afloat and under way, delivering only cockles of marketable size into the hold by suction. Four hours of this dredging can usually gather as many cockles as were gathered by hand in eight hours, and on beds with a plentiful supply a ton can be dredged in an hour with a crew of two men, resulting in some damage to the beds, though, sadly, this is now regarded as acceptable.

Overleaf: Fig. 41. The second stage in the evolution of the cockle boat. In the foreground a Leigh cockler of about 1930 passes one of the original sailing cocklers. By about 1930 the boats had become motor craft with a cutter rig of modest proportions.

Fig. 40. Unloading cockles at Leigh around 1902. The method of unloading remained unchanged for at least a century. A succession of fishermen carried two loaded baskets hooked to short lengths of rope hanging from each end of a wooden yoke carried on their shoulders. The baskets were filled in the hold and were carried at a smart pace up to the cockle shed of the boat's owner. A number of sheds lined the sea wall path to the west of the village. There the cockles were cooked, originally in hot water but in later years by steam. The shells were separated from the meat by sieving and the meat was then sold directly across a counter to passers-by or was sent away by road or rail for sale elsewhere, much of it going to the nearby resort of Southend.

In this photograph a carvel-planked cockle boat lies aground in the foreground, and a counter-sterned smack is in the background. The craft in the centre of the photograph is a "cockle galley", one of the many old warship's boat, which were bought cheaply from Chatham or Sheerness dockyards by Leigh fishermen. Some of these were already fitted with a centreplate, others had a wooden false keel added to provide some windward ability. They were rigged as a gaff sloop, mostly with a boomless mainsail in the manner of a bawley. Usually they remained open boats. This is believed to be the only photograph of one of these craft, which were the forerunners of the fine fleet of specially built sailing and then motor cocklers working from Leigh.

Fig. 42. Leigh cocklers racing before 1914. Although similar in appearance to the larger bawleys these were smaller craft and because of their work had a draught of hull of about 2 feet 6 inches to 3 feet against the 5 feet to 6 feet 6 inches of the bawleys. Cocklers needed to take the ground to allow their crews to scatter around the boat and rake up the catch, which was tipped into the hold, where the large centreboard case acted as a shifting board to prevent the cargo moving. The early craft used for cockling from Leigh were a nondescript collection and included several ex-naval ship's boats which led to the nickname "cockle galleys". The *Alice and Florrie* was a typical Leigh cockler built in 1905 by S. J. Peters at Leigh. She was 30 feet long by 10 feet beam and drew 3 feet 3 inches, extending to about 6 feet with the centreplate lowered. She was carvel planked on sawn oak frames with some intermediate bent timbers. She could sail at about 5 knots in favourable conditions and was typical of her type. She was converted to a yacht in 1935 and is still sailing from Fambridge, on the River Crouch.

These cocklers are setting spinnakers in a light wind and have yard topsails set. They also fly a flag on the fore topmast stay, in the manner of the contemporary Thames barge race competitors.

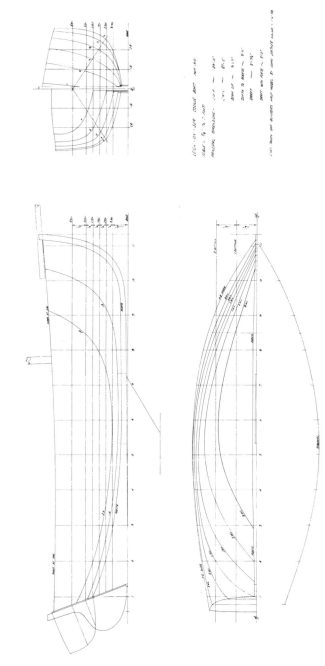

Fig. 43. Lines of a Leigh cockle boat built about 1910 taken from a half model by the author. Principal dimensions are 29 feet length overall, 27 feet 2 inches waterline length by 9 feet 7 inches beam and 2 feet 7½ inches hull draught. Draught with centreplate lowered was 5 feet. The bow is fairly fine and the forefoot well rounded. The run and after sections are well formed and altogether the boat probably sailed well.

Above: Fig. 44. Cockles are raked from the sands with two rakes. First a steel rake was used to drag the cockles out over an area at around arm's length. Then a wooden rake having closely spaced teeth was used to bring them together in a slurry of sand and water. The netful was then washed in a pool and was tipped into one of a pair of wicker baskets that each cockler had with him. When full the baskets were hooked on to ropes suspended from a wooden yoke and carried quickly back to the cockle boat. A simple stage was usually rigged by the side of the boat to give a foothold for the cockler to lift the baskets to deck level and then tip them into the hold.
Raking of cockles started when the boats grounded and the tide had fallen sufficiently for the men to rake. They might work for four hours or so, with a brief interval for a meal and then continue until the tide flooded enough to stop work. Several tons of cockles might be gathered in that time with a crew of perhaps four men. The boats waited until there was sufficient water to enable them to be sailed, then made their way back to Leigh. Cockling in this way was much more tiring work than it appeared. During recent years this method has been superseded by use of suction dredge equipment mounted on the boats, which needs a crew of only two to operate.

Overleaf: Fig. 45. A view of the busy beach to the east of Southend Pier around 1910. The boats in the foreground are two of George Murrell's sailing lifeboats filling with a freight of trippers for a sail. Murrell bought an old beach yawl from Norfolk to carry trippers off the beach. She was popular and he soon had other boats built in the same style, as here, with a gaff mainsail, some with boom, foresail and a jib and a mizzen which was usually a lug. At least four of these boats operated. The left background shows the dome of the Kursaal pleasure ground near which was the yard of Hayward, who built most of the beach boats for Southend. In the right background are sailing barges at the Corporation jetty. The boarding gangways are run out at the bow of each boat and the crew stand ready, while on the promenade their mates exhort the visitors to "Come along now! Sail in the lifeboat".

77

SAILING YACHTS, SOUTHEND-ON-SEA.

CHAPTER SIX

Smacks

THE sailing smacks of the county of Essex evolved through many centuries and their exact origins are now almost impossible to discover. They were built, owned and fished from small ports on the rivers Colne, Blackwater, Crouch and Roach, with others from Harwich and Leigh.

Basically the Essex smack was a cutter-rigged fishing vessel having various forms and dimensions for different fisheries. There were three principal types in the nineteenth and early twentieth centuries. Small smacks, up to about 35 feet and about 12 tons register, were mainly used for estuary dredging and trawling. Some 12 to 18 tonners, up to about 50 feet, were used for this work at times, but were mainly fishing coastwise and at sea, spratting and oystering, dredging five-fingers (starfish) and mussels at times, and fish trawling. Largest of all were the seagoing smacks up to about 65 feet in length and 20 tons register or more, which were principally owned in the River Colne and at Burnham, the Colne boats fishing far afield. All were noted for windward ability, seaworthiness and speed.

Several hundred smacks were sailing from Essex by the early nineteenth century, the majority owned at Brightlingsea, an ancient small town on a creek at the mouth of the river Colne and a "limb" of the Cinque Port of Sandwich. Brightlingsea fishermen dredged oysters in the Colne estuary and coastwise and also deep sea oysters and scallops where these could be found around the British Isles and off the coast of France and Holland. They spratted with the stow net in winter, trawled and carried fish, and salvaged from the large number of wrecks off the east coast in the days of merchant sail. Brightlingsea shipyards built many hundreds of smacks and small wooden ships. Its seaman took to professional yachting and achieved a great reputation until this important summer aspect of Essex seafaring ended in 1939.

Six miles up the wooded, winding Colne lies the author's native village of Rowhedge—for centuries the home of an adventurous maritime community of about 1000: fishermen, professional yachtsmen, shipbuilders and masters and sailors of small ships. Its mellowed buildings looked on a waterside which stirred briskly each high water with a fleet of sixty smacks, many large cutters, ranging all round the British Isles, to Ireland, France, Norway and the Baltic in the same fishing trades as the Brightlingsea men. Rowhedge was the home of many noted racing yachtsmen. Its seamen gained international fame as professional yacht skippers and crews from before 1800 until 1939. Rowhedge captains skippered four challengers for the America's Cup, besides scores of other large yachts and hundreds of smaller ones. Hundreds of its sailors formed their crews. The village shipyards built ships, yachts and smacks.

On the opposite riverbank lies Wivenhoe, a larger village, which owned fewer smacks but had a fleet of merchant brigs, barquentines and schooners, and shipyards building smacks, yachts and small ships. Wivenhoe men were also yacht captains and crews. Tollesbury, on the nearby river Blackwater, was a fishing community owning about 40 smacks under twenty tons in the coastal spratting, trawling and inshore oyster-dredging trades. After 1890 Tollesbury men were also taken on in the racing yachts; at first as hands, some later to become captains and racing skippers. West Mersea, on a creek at the west end of Mersea Island, had little interest beyond the estuary of the Blackwater after the mid-nineteenth century. Its 55 or so small smacks worked the extensive estuary oyster fisheries, where sail survived until 1939. Most of the surviving smack-yachts have originated from Mersea and several still moor there.

Bradwell, on the opposite shore of the Blackwater, was a rural parish owning a few small smacks which were moored in its creek, used by barges and wildfowlers in season. Maldon, at the head of the navigable Blackwater twelve miles upstream, owned a score of little river and estuary smacks, but numbers of small coasting and seagoing merchant sailing ships and barges were built and owned there. Further south, on the River Crouch, the ancient town of Burnham owned about a score of big cutter smacks in the same trades as those from Brightlingsea and Rowhedge; these there were besides large numbers of small smacks, dredging the extensive oyster layings in the Crouch and Roach rivers, and a score or so small smacks from the village of Paglesham on the Roach.

Harwich, the premier seaport of Essex, had many smacks in the deep-sea cod trade, often sailing to Iceland on venturesome long-lining voyages and regularly fishing in the North Sea. There were also several big cutter smacks spratting, fish trawling and salvaging, and boarding and landing pilots. After the mid-nineteenth century Harwich fishermen took to shrimping and developed the bawley type, which was also used at Leigh in greater numbers and at Whitstable, Faversham, Gravesend and the Medway.

Essex shipbuilders were producing fine-lined fast cutters well before 1800, but bluff-bowed, clench-planked cutter smacks were in common use into the early nineteenth century. The larger ones had lute sterns, an early form of counter, and many of the smaller had transom sterns. Indicative of their shape and proportions is the little *Boadicea*, built at Maldon in 1809 and still sailing. Carvel planking was introduced, probably during the eighteenth century, possibly earlier, although clench building remained common into the early nineteenth century. The earliest recorded smack having carvel planking was the Wivenhoe owned *Tribune*, built at Ipswich in 1836, but it is certain that there were many much earlier built in this way. By the mid-nineteenth century the

Essex cutter smack had been perfected, principally by builders on the River Colne, who were much influenced in design after the seventeen-eighties by their close association with the builders of fast yachts. These were manned by local seamen who readily adopted, and demanded, unusually fast and weatherly hull forms and sail plans. Thus the design of yachts and smacks had early interacted and Philip Sainty of Wivenhoe, who had a shipyard there, and earlier at Brightlingsea and Colchester, was a noted builder of both until his death in 1837. The Harris family, Enos and Peter, of Rowhedge, built over 60 smacks there including many large cutters and ketches between 1840 and 1875 and a few thereafter, along with many yachts. A Mr Cheek built there in earlier times.

At Brightlingsea the Aldous family built large numbers of smacks of all sizes and types and others were launched there by Root and Diaper. Later small smacks were built by John James and by Douglas Stone and Sons, who built the last one, the *Peace*, launched on the Colne in 1909. Some large smacks were built at Ipswich by Read and Page and later by Thomas Harvey and Son, whose Wivenhoe shipyard, succeeding the business of Philip Sainty, produced many shapely and well-finished smacks. Typical of these was the fifteen ton *Beatrice*, launched in 1848 for a Captain Mason of Wivenhoe and later owned by the author's grandfather, Captain James Barnard of Rowhedge. Her dimensions were 52 feet length overall, 45 feet registered length, by 12 foot beam by 6 foot 6 inches draught aft. The plumb stem, slightly rounded forefoot, long rocking keel, great forward freeboard and graceful sheer sweeping to a low, well-proportioned counter distinguish the type with different builders. Hull lines varied in detail but typically the hull had considerable rise of floor, a moderately firm bilge, hollow bow waterlines and a long and beautifully fair run to the flat-sectioned counter.

These vessels had inherent speed to windward and the bold bow kept them going in a sea, but their low after freeboard and the fifteen-inch-high bulwarks necessary for handling fishing gear made them wet aft in bad weather, when they could stand extremely hard driving. All ballast was inside, of shingle and iron pigs ceiled over. From forward the hull was divided into a fo'c'sle store for paints, sails and ropes, entered by a deck hatch. The fish hold amidships was bulkheaded off at the mast and from the cabin aft. It was served by a 5-foot-square main hatch, with a small spratting hatch adjacent so that the cod end of the net could be progressively shot down it without exposing too large an opening in winter sea conditions. The crew's quarters for four were in the cabin aft, with cupboard bunks around the sides and a coal stove for warmth and cooking. The cabin hatch was immediately forward of the tiller and the compass was mounted inside it for protection. On deck a handspike windlass handled the chain cable and an iron, geared hand capstan the trawl warps. Halyards and sheets were brought in by hand.

Like all of her kind the *Beatrice* was rigged as a true cutter, with long housing topmast and the bowsprit housing between deck bitts, one of which was reinforced with a knee, the other fitted to the keelson and also bearing a pawl for the windlass. The *Beatrice* set 1,250 square feet in the mainsail, foresail (staysail), jib and the jib-headed topsail. In light weather a larger yard topsail was set, besides a balloon staysail or a balloon jib or "bowsprit spinnaker" from the bowsprit end, sheeted well abaft the shrouds when fetching on the wind or boomed out when running. A small jib and a storm jib completed the usual sail outfit. A trysail was not usually carried in smacks of this size but the mainsail had a close reef. Until about 1890 such smacks were built for £10 per registered ton for hull, mast and spars. Construction was simple but strong: English elm keel, pine keelson, English oak centreline and sawn frames, pitch-pine bottom planking and often Baltic fir side planking with English oak sheer, wale and bilge strakes, though some, like the *Beatrice*, were planked throughout in oak. All fastenings were iron. Deck beams were English oak and deck planking pine. The deck shelf, mast and spars were also of pine.

These smacks were well kept, clean and able, each representing one man's investment and pride, manned by himself, his sons, relatives and neighbours, all fishing on a system of shares from the proceeds of the catch.

Dredging oysters was one of the principal occupations of Essex smacks. The iron-framed dredges were shaped like a capital A, with a three foot hoeing bar across its feet. A short net of twine spread from the hoe, crosspiece and sides between and had a chain-mesh bottom and a stick to square its after end. The apex of the iron frame was swelled and had an iron ring forged in it, to which a bass warp was made fast to tow the dredge (see fig. 90). A sailing smack might tow from four to eight such dredges across an oyster ground, gathering, besides oysters, much rubbish and pests such as limpets, from which the marketable oysters had to be culled, the rubbish being thrown overboard. Pests such as slipper limpets were kept on deck to be dumped ashore when the day's work was done, an unceasing struggle to keep the grounds clear.

All hauling of dredges was done by hand; the work required sailing craft that handled well, sometimes under sail which was reduced to control speed to suit the conditions of wind and tide, often in confined waters and amongst numbers of other smacks similarly manoeuvring. Such work improved the smartness of the Essex seamen. Between 30 and 100 smacks of up to 15 tons dredged the Colne estuary fishery, administered by the Colchester Oyster Fishery Company, which had strong links with the Corporation of Colchester, the port at the navigable head of the river. The dredgermen in the Colne had to be Freemen of the river Colne, a privilege much prized in those days of scarce winter employment. The nearby Blackwater and Crouch rivers had extensive oyster layings worked by companies, but without the system of Freemen.

For several centuries oyster dredging at sea was also carried on by Essex smacks. Smacks from the Colne were venturing down Channel in the early eighteenth century and probably earlier. In 1736 they were recorded as taking brood oysters in the Fal and bringing them back to be laid in the Colne for fattening. At the same time French oysters were being imported from Cancale to Rochester, Faversham, Colchester and Maldon in large quantities, affecting the east coast fishermen's trade. Nevertheless the oyster fisheries remained Brightlingsea's greatest industry throughout the eighteenth century, and between 1776 and 1806 the Colne fleet of smacks increased by half. These ranged from 14 to 40 tons, many being built at Brightlingsea and others at Rowhedge and Wivenhoe. They then cost about £10 per registered ton for the hull, and a 20 ton smack cost about £180 to equip. These craft were expected to last thirty to forty years employed in fishing. They were manned by two to four men. In spring, in those days they went dredging off the coasts of Hampshire and Dorset, while at home as many as 130 smacks were once counted working at one time in sight of East Mersea.

Oyster dredging continued to be the mainstay of Brightlingsea and the Colne villages into the mid-nineteenth century. In 1848 about 180 smacks of 15 to 40 tons were owned at Brightlingsea, about sixty at Rowhedge and a smaller number at Wivenhoe. Sixty or so smacks went annually from the Colne in February and March to Jersey in the Channel Islands and to Falmouth, where they continued dredging for oysters for two or three months before returning home. At that time Brightlingsea Creek was lined with large numbers of oyster layings where the fishermen laid the sprat and young brood which were gathered in the Colne and Blackwater and often elsewhere until they were grown to marketable size. Then they were sold in quantities to Kentish fishermen, to be relaid in beds around Whitstable and the Swale for fattening and eventually sale to London.

The oyster dredgers suffered from the severe winters and also from vagaries of sprat falls, when young oysters are produced literally in millions, but with very high mortality. However, until the eighteen-seventies the numbers of smacks and men employed in dredging continually increased, despite occasional fatal frosts when ice in the rivers and creeks killed hundreds of thousands of oysters in the Colne, the Blackwater and along the Kent coast. The trade continued to flourish, and by 1861 there were about 200 smacks working from Brightlingsea alone, with some increase also at Rowhedge and Wivenhoe.

The fishing trade expanded considerably in the mid-nineteenth century as a result of railways reaching north-east Essex. At Wivenhoe, a first effect of the arrival of the railway was to encourage the landing of sprats for distribution by rail as field manure, besides giving speedy access to Billingsgate and other markets for prime fish such as spring soles or boxed smoked sprats in winter. Rumours of an extension to Brightlingsea opened rosier prospects, with the solution of the fish-marketing problem by a rail service available where the majority of the smacks landed catches, without having to work tides to

Wivenhoe. Grimsby and Lowestoft had been developed by the railway companies during the previous ten years, growing from insignificant villages into huge fishing ports. Who knew what might develop at Brightlingsea when the railway reached there in 1866? The golden dream was never realised; the capital was lacking, though not the enterprise. Meanwhile the deep-sea dredging of oysters by smacks from the Colne and elsewhere continued. In the eighteen-sixties oysters were in demand and were being discovered in large quantities by the smacks. Dredging went on off Orfordness, off Ostend in Belgium, in parts of the English Channel and around Jersey, which became a busy centre. Colne yards were building smacks as fast as possible to reap this harvest, and on one occasion at Brightlingsea four smacks were launched in one day.

Emboldened by optimism, many smacksmen who had money to venture placed orders for new craft, of a size which had not before been owned locally nor in such numbers. No companies were created, for the thought of skippering smacks owned by others, common in other ports, was horrifying to the vigorously independent Essexmen, who especially wished to develop their long established dredging of sea-oysters.

The result was a fleet of powerful cutters, with a glorious sheer and rakish rig. Almost all were designed and built in local yards, with the exception of a few constructed at the Channel Islands port of Gorey, Jersey, then a noted centre of the shellfish industry and much frequented by Essexmen. Aldous of Bright-lingsea built thirty-six of these big smacks between 1857 and 1867. Harris at Rowhedge and Harvey at Wivenhoe built a good number and some were launched on the Blackwater. These smacks of between 20 and 40 registered tons dwarfed the little estuary oyster dredgers, and there was as great a difference between them in purpose and voyaging as that between a deep-sea trawler and an inshore fisherman of today.

The Rowhedge-owned *Aquiline*, belonging to Captain Harry Cook, was typical. A bold-sheered cutter of 21 registered tons, she was launched from the Harris yard in 1865, where her 65 foot hull was well built and finely formed. It had a beam of 15 feet and drew 8 feet 6 inches when loaded to her hold capacity. She carried a sail area of about 2000 square feet in her working canvas. The mainboom was 45 feet long and the bowsprit 25 feet outboard. When dredging at sea the mainsail was often handed and the mainboom was stowed in a crutch, a large trysail being set in its place, sheeted by tackles to the quarters.

The arrangements of these larger smacks differed greatly from the small smacks that still survive for pleasure sailing. Forward, the usual handspike windlass handled the anchor cable, which ran out clear of the stem on a short wooden davit. In season, it also handled the stowboat gear. A large geared hand-winch, having four barrels, was fitted immediately forward of the mast for working halyards, running out the bowsprit, working fishing gear or whipping out the cargo. A winch or geared hand-capstan stood amidships and could be worked by two or more men when dredging or working trawl warps. All were hauled by muscle power, as, unlike the specialised trawling smacks from the large fishing ports, which were equipped with steam capstans, the Essex boats relied solely on "Armstrong's Patent" to work their fishing gear, a feature they endured until the eclipse of sail. A clinker-planked boat from 13 to 15 feet long was carried on deck or was lashed upside down over the main hatch in foul weather. In port on Sundays or on regatta days most of these smacks sported a long masthead pennant emblazoned with the smack's name or initial. Many had signal letters alloted to them, which is proof of their varied sea work. Few had channels for the shrouds, as these interfered with boarding stowboat gear.

Below deck the forepeak was a cable locker and abaft this was the mast room, as the space between the peak bulkhead and mast was called. This housed a large scuttle-butt for drinking water and racks for bread and vegetable stores. Partial bulkheads set this off from the main hold, which occupied about one third of the smack's length. Ballast was clean beach shingle with a proportion of iron pigs, covered by a wood ceiling. All hands berthed in the cabin aft, entered by a companion hatch in the deck. In this space of perhaps fourteen by nine feet six men lived for weeks at a time. Locker seats ran down each side. The four bunks lined the sides, behind the lockers, each having sliding panels which could be closed by the occupant to shut himself off for sleep or from his noisy mates. A big double berth across the counter was known as the Yarmouth Roads and could hold two apprentices, who were lulled to sleep by the rudder's groan and kick in the trunk near their heads. On the black coal stove a kettle simmered and a large teapot warmed, only emptied when it would no longer hold six mugfuls of water. Knives and forks were stuck in cracks of the deck beams and saucepan lids were used as plates in a seaway with the handle gripped between the knees.

These craft formed the most adventurous fleet of fishing vessels ever to sail from Essex. However, there is no sense in attempting to glamourise the fisheries in which they took part, which were always hard, often dangerous and usually miserably rewarding financially, but they bred men of strong and independent character. Theirs was not the comparatively idyllic life of the estuary dredgers, but a thrusting existence, where they had to be alive to any and every opportunity that came their way. Most skippers began as apprentices, serving on board their master's smack and living in his house when in port. These boys were sometimes at sea at the age of twelve, being bound for from five to seven years to the smack owner, who might have two apprentices serving on board his smack. This system existed in the seventeenth century but died out by the end of the nineteenth. The owner found them food, but the apprentice supplied their own favourite rig of cheesecutter cap, white canvas jumper and smock over a thick guernsey. Stout duffle trousers were tucked into leather sea-boots, which had cobbled soles, often studded with wooden pegs for a better grip on deck.

It was a life which produced competent seamen and if the boy was lucky offered prospects of advancement within the harsh framework of the times. The boys were drawn from a variety of origins, many from families unconnected with seafaring. There seem to have been few unfortunate orphans or reformatory school children shipped in the Essex smacks, unlike those sailing from the large trawling ports such as Yarmouth, Grimsby, Hull and Lowestoft. Most were local Essex boys who were often sons or relatives of the smack owner and opted for a life afloat, or could find nothing ashore in those times of widespread poverty in agriculture. Typical of this time was Joseph Theobald, who was born in the rural parish of Fingringhoe by the Colne in 1827, son of Jacob Theobald, husbandman. After working for two years on the farm Joseph was apprenticed in September 1843 to James Mothersole, a smack owner of nearby Rowhedge (East Donyland parish). He was bound apprentice for four and a half years "to be taught, learned and informed in the art, trade or business of a mariner or seaman with the circumstances thereto belonging, and [James Mothersole] shall and will find and provide for the said apprentice sufficient meat, drink and lodging, and the said James Mothersole doth covenant and agree to pay unto the said apprentice the sum of thirty-five pounds of lawful money . . . and also to pay half the subscription for a surgeon for the said apprentice in case of sickness. And the said Jacob Theobald (the father) covenants and agrees to find for the said apprentice washing and mending and all manner of sea bedding, wearing apparel and other necessaries . . ."

Joseph took to sea life and having completed his apprenticeship was by 1853 mate of the 72 ton cargo vessel *Rapid*, but in the manner of those times and small ships, he served variously as mate, seaman, AB and bosun in a variety of brigs, brigantines, smacks and ketches, besides several yachts. He voyaged around the British coasts, to the Continent and to the Baltic, becoming a certificated mate in 1858 and sailing from Rowhedge into the eighteen-seventies, after which it seems he came ashore, and became a partner in the business of Francis and Theobald, sprat and five finger merchants of Rowhedge during the eighteen-eighties. His son James carried on the seafaring tradition in smacks and yachts and his grandson was a respected Rowhedge shipwright. A typical family sequence of the times.

There was little of the by guess and by God style of navigation amongst these smacks' confident skippers, most of whom were progressive enough to obtain a Fishing Master's certificate when these were introduced in the eighteen-seventies. Their quest for oysters and scallops led them at various times to work the Inner Dowsing and the Dudgeon banks, landing catches at Grimsby or Blakeney in north Norfolk, the Ness grounds, stretching from Orfordness to Cromer in Norfolk the Galloper and Kentish Knock areas of the North Sea, and the Terschelling and Hinder banks off the Dutch coast, landing catches at Brightlingsea. In the English Channel they dredged the Goodwin, Sandettie and the Varne grounds besides those on the French coast at Caen Bay, Dieppe, St

Valéry-sur-Somme, Fécamp, Calais and Dunkirk, using Ramsgate, Dover, Shoreham or Newhaven to land catches. Down Channel, West Bay provided some work and occasionally the Cornish Fal and Helford rivers were visited by the Essexmen, while the Channel Island of Jersey attracted large numbers of Essex and other smacks to its fishery for seventy years. Others sailed round Land's End to work on the south Pembrokeshire coast, based at Swansea and Bangor, and southern Ireland, north west Ireland and the Solway Firth regularly saw the rakish Colne topmasts.

When dredging, work aboard these smacks was hard. On the grounds the topmast was often struck and a reef tucked in the mainsail, or the trysail would be set to ease speed and motion in a seaway and keep the boom clear of unwary heads. After this they worked almost continuously day and night, with only occasional spells for mugs of tea and a bite to eat. It was muscle-cracking work winding up the big sea dredges with six foot hoeing edges from 26 fathoms by hand. Often six were worked at a time on 65 fathom, 3 inch bass warps, leading in through multiple rollers on the rail or through a port in the bulwark. Each weary foot of it was cranked home, with one man keeping tension on the slack, which jerked back on every sea to etch new scars into hands already torn by the tiny shell picked up by the warp. So it went on hour after hour, without even the respite of sorting between hauls which trawling gives. At about 3 am the gear would be laid in and the crew took half-hour watches before recommencing at six; this might go on for five or six days.

Hard as they were the fisheries flourished and by 1874 there were 132 first-class smacks of 15 to 30 tons registered at Colchester, in addition to 250 second-class of under 15 tons and 40 third-class vessels. By far the largest part of these were owned at Brightlingsea, with Rowhedge accounting for 29 first-class smacks, Wivenhoe 12 and Tollesbury 8. Few of these large smacks were owned by West Mersea fishermen, whose interests were chiefly centred in the Blackwater oyster fisheries, and although some had made ventures further afield in earlier times, there were none owned there in the later days.

Rich oyster beds were discovered by the big smacks off Jersey in 1787 and the news travelled fast, for within a few months over 300 smacks from Essex, Shoreham, Emsworth and Faversham, manned by two thousand men, were working there. In a few months the quiet port of Gorey became a boom town. Later, a fleet of 60 Essex smacks sailed there each spring and carried on dredging the waters despite the hazards of the Napoleonic wars. The Jersey fishery declined during the eighteen-forties and became exhausted by 1871.

Wherever there were oysters the far ranging Essexmen would find them, and flourishing local oyster fisheries at Swansea and Cardigan Bays in Wales, Largo Bay in Fife, Scotland, in the Solway Firth and off north Norfolk were rapidly worked out by fleets of Colne smacks, to the rage, and often despite the resistance, of local fishermen. Sea oysters were also dredged on the Terschelling bank off the Dutch coast, about 112 miles east from Orfordness, from which point the smacks made their departure. Trips averaged twelve days, during which a haul of ten thousand large oysters could be expected. This was a harsh fishery, a lee shore in prevailing winds, with no handy leeward refuge. Many Colne smacks and their crews were lost off Terschelling and elsewhere in those adventurous times. In a January gale in 1891 the Brightlingsea smack *Glance*, sailed by Captain Tom Tillett, and the *Gemini*, John Causton master, were lost with all hands, and in a period of about three years there were twelve hands lost overboard from Colne smacks when fishing.

Apart from these activities many Colne smacks were employed on contract for £12 per week as fish carriers for the lumbering Grimsby, Yarmouth, Hull and Lowestoft ketches that trawled the North Sea in fleets. The Colne boats were ideal for this work, being fast and capable of driving through foul weather. Blow high or low they usually got to London's Billingsgate fish market before the iced cargo had turned.

Colne smacks were also employed in the seasonal carrying of fresh salmon from the western Irish ports of Sligo and Westport, around the northern tip of Ireland to the Liverpool market. This was a voyage which was exposed to the full sweep and fury of the north Atlantic and most smacks in this trade took the precaution of reeving chain reef-pendants to stand the hard driving of a four-day round voyage to Liverpool, no mean feat for such small ships.

The Rowhedge *New Unity*, a 39 tonner, owned by the author's great grandfather, Captain Thomas Barnard, the noted salvager, was one of several Colne smacks engaged at times in the equally arduous voyages to German and other Baltic ports with barrelled herring, shipped from Stornoway in the Western Isles of Scotland. During the eighteen-sixties and -seventies several Rowhedge smacks were chartered by Trinity House as pilot tenders for the Harwich station. These included the *Young Pheasant* owned by Samuel Mills; *Deer Hound*, Orlando Lay; *Thomas and Mary*, Thomas Barnard; *Beulah*, Daniel James; *Increase*, John Glover; and *Scout*, Harvey Carder. This work was much sought as an assured basic income and consisted mainly of landing pilots from ships outward bound from Harwich. But when the chance of a profitable salvage job or good fishing occurred, these smacks often went missing from their pilotage duties, to the consternation of Trinity House. In fact there was little these smacksmen could not or would not do to get a living. Many were in the cattle trade from the Channel Islands to Weymouth at certain times of the year. The Brightlingsea smack *Glibe* was typical, being licensed to carry nineteen swine in the hold and two cows on deck, where the boy had to trice up the boom to clear their backs when going about.

Another trade carried on at times by several Brightlingsea smacks was the carriage of explosives, which at the time were often not entrusted to steamships. In 1886 William Pannell, who was a partner with E. A. Hibbs in a sailmaking business in the town, bought the 18 ton smack *Waterlily*, which was sailed by his brother in law, John Ainger, for stowboating in winter, at which she did well. Like many of her contemporaries she also did a little coasting, carrying explosives and small arms to the Continent. She also put in a season's scallop dredging in the English Channel under Captain Ben Wenlock of Brightlingsea. The Rowhedge *Aquiline* and *New Blossom* were often employed in the spring potato trade from St Malo and St Michels in France to Colchester, and Charles Crosby's *New Blossom* frequently shipped the Rowhedge village coal from Shields, besides sometimes voyaging to the Baltic with coal or barrelled herrings, before the eighteen-eighties. Others, like the big Brightlingsea smack *Vanduara*, carried dynamite from Continental ports and earned high freights for the dangerous cargo.

The big Colne smacks held an annual race in the eighteen-seventies and eighteen-eighties with a hogshead of beer as a prize. This event, which died out in the eighteen-eighties, was quite distinct from the annual regatta struggles amongst their smaller sisters. The deep-sea smacksmen scorned an inshore course, though the start and finish were in the Colne. Racing was out around the Galloper Light Vessel and return. If they got a fair wind home then the great half-squaresails, carried before spinnakers were devised, ranted them home into the Colne, the winner promptly fixing a metal cock at the topmast head as the finishing gun boomed from a committee boat off East Mersea Stone, announcing the Cock of the Fleet for the year.

In the latter half of the nineteenth century yachting rivalled and then eclipsed the Essex deep-sea fisheries as a living and the smaller 12 to 18 ton smacks became popular for working the Thames estuary and its approaches, as these could be more economically laid up all summer while their crews made more colourful sailing history.

The days of the big smacks were ending, although as late as 1890 Brightlingsea had a fleet of fifty-two. Twelve years later a series of poisoning scares killed the demand for sea oysters and the remaining fleet took to working down Channel from January to March, usually dredging from French ports, notably Boulogne, and sending the catch to London by night steamer and rail. Shoreham was also used when dredging grounds off Beachy Head, and in the mid-nineteenth century many Colne smacks gathered there to work. As late as 1903 Colne smacks were dredging oysters on the Ridge and the Varne shoals, using Newhaven in Sussex as a base, but little or no money was made from all this endeavour and hard work.

Scallops became another shellfish sought by the Essex smacks and others from south coast ports. Only small scallops called queens, about 3 inches in diameter, were dredged on the Essex and Kent coasts, but there were larger ones averaging 4½ to 5 inches in diameter to be found in the English Channel, from Dover westwards and particularly off Hastings and Worthing in Sussex. This attracted only 3 smacks in the early 1850s, rising to 20 five years later. In 1877 40 smacks from the Colne, Dover, Rye and Folkestone were dredging scallops and these were sent to London in large quantities and were also sold locally. The Colne smacks sought the scallop further afield on the French coast, the Channel Islands and off the Dutch coast. In 1899 there were ten first class smacks from Brightlingsea dredging scallops there from January to late March, and this continued with varying success until 1914. It was for a time briefly revived after 1919 by a few remaining large smacks and motor craft, and there were also occasional attempts to revive the oyster and scallop dredging in Caen Bay and elsewhere in the Channel, culminating in 1948 when a motor fishing vessel was fitted out at Brightlingsea under Frank Goodwin, one of the last of the Colne men to combine fishing with serving on yachts in the old tradition, but he found little to dredge.

The 1914–18 war dealt a great blow to the big smacks; although fish prices were high, several were sold away to Lowestoft and elsewhere, while others worked on government fishing contracts, mainly stowboating for sprats. After the war a remnant carried on in the traditional ways, supplemented by a few motor drifters bought from other ports. With the exception of these and half a dozen paddle steam dredgers owned by oyster companies at Burnham and in the Colne, steam found no place in the Essex fishing fleet.

In these days of well-buoyed fairways and elaborate navigational aids it is difficult to picture the appalling conditions which existed for coastwise shipping during the early and mid nineteenth century. Most trade was carried on in unhandy and often ill-found square-rigged vessels and there were few lifeboats or licensed pilots. It was not surprising that ships were driven ashore in dozens during an average winter gale. The Colne smacks, in common with the Harwich-men, were quick to seize salvage opportunities, and until the eighteen-eighties Receivers of Wreck on the Essex coast had a busy time. Customs warehouses were crammed with salvaged goods, as were many smacksmen's cellars. The spars, equipment and even hulls of wrecked and refloated vessels were regularly being brought in, advertised in the press and auctioned. This work, with the lifesaving it often entailed, was known in Essex as salvaging.

Captain Thomas Barnard of Rowhedge, the author's great grandfather, was among the most noted salvagers and lifesavers, with his big smacks *Thomas and Mary*, and later the *New Unity*. Throughout his career, until he retired from sea in 1881, he saved over nine hundred lives without the loss of any of his crews. His seamanship was typical of the Swin rangers, as the old Colne salvagers liked to style themselves. They were bred to sail and learned to handle it from boyhood, learning the hardest way by fishing the treacherous old North Sea. Ranging the death-trap shoals for whatever luckless ship the sea might bring, they possessed a courage born from a calculated knowledge of the sea. They were hard, fiercely independent and quick as gulls to seize any chance the sea brought when fishing or salvaging. They frequently risked lives, smacks and livelihoods to take off shipwrecked crews in the foulest weather.

Salvage work was profitable as well as heroic. The fisheries were frequently depressed and salvage presented heaven-sent chances for bolstering earnings. News of a well-laden wreck spread fast and crowds of mariners thronged village watersides, eager to be taken on as extra hands aboard the salt-rimed smacks already discharging salvaged cargo. To help in this work the salvagers devised special tools; in winter most large smacks carried a variety of grapnels, mauls, crowbars, axes, tackles, extra warps and fenders. Salvaged cargoes ranged from the usual coal, timber and general goods to the fabulous cargo of the Knock John Ship of 1856, a German vessel which stranded on the Knock Sand bound for China with barter goods. The wreck was first boarded by a Brightlingsea smack and from it they took the richest haul ever made on the east coast.

During the early nineteenth century smack crews might be awarded as much as £80 each for salvaging a small vessel such as a sloop or a brig, and for larger ships sums of £500 were sometimes recorded. Successful salvaging meant big money in contemporary values. For saving life the salvagers expected no reward, but many received medals from humane societies and from British and foreign governments, besides tokens such as inscribed telescopes or binoculars. One rescue will illustrate their work.

Beating out to the Kentish Knock one wild and bitter night, Thomas Barnard found a large German barque, crowded with emigrants bound for New York, beating her bottom out on the sands in the roaring gale. No time could be lost if all were to be saved. Manoeuvring alongside in heavy seas, they bundled the terrified passengers over from the doomed ship to the wildly pitching smack. It was not until the *New Unity* had made three passages to Walton and others to a steamer which had hove to nearby that the ship's complement of over two hundred were saved from the splendid barque, which was matchwood forty-eight hours later.

On the Colne the period from 1860 to 1914 was an era of great expansion and growing fame in professional yachting, for the Essex smacks were the finest school for teaching the subtleties of handling fore- and aft-rigged craft in confined waters and under competitive conditions of workaday sailing. Most of the great yacht-racing skippers sprang from this source, which also trained hundreds of smart hands until the decline of working sail and of the need for professional yacht hands in the late nineteen-thirties. Many fine, fast smacks of 15 to 18 tons register were built from the often large sums of prize money won by the Colne skippers of racing yachts. Their lean cutters were principally intended for winter spratting and fish trawling and were of a size which could be inexpensively maintained in use and also economically laid up during the summer yachting season. Most of them bore names of the yachts whose smart handling had financed their construction. Just as Colne-built smacks and revenue cutters had influenced yacht design during the early nineteenth century, so in later decades the local association with the handling and development of the racing yacht affected smack design. Although ability to earn a living in the winter fisheries always remained a prime consideration when building smacks, and few if any were specially built for racing in the annual regattas, refinements in hull-form and rig were continuous and the weatherlines and speed desirable in the fisheries led to the launch of fine cutters from the Colne and Blackwater yards.

In September, when the yachts laid up, crowding the rivers, mud-berths, the greater number of their crews were soon busy seeking winter employment. Most "took on in the stowboaters", as smacks engaged in the winter spratting were called. Some took the train for London or Southampton docks, seeking berths in foreign-bound steamers for six months. But the smacks remained the winter mainstay, for there was little else, and thirty to forty stowboaters annually fitted out from Rowhedge to join the total including scores from Brightlingsea, and others from Wivenhoe, and from Tollesbury, the only Blackwater village to participate in the spratting, although the West Mersea smack *Priscilla* joined in for a few seasons.

Autumn high spring tides saw smacks floated from their summer berths to lay on the hards, which resounded all day long with the ring of caulking irons and the chaff of seamen bending canvas, rigging gear and painting and tarring hulls. Along the shore roads men bore on their shoulders the great stow nets and their cumbersome wooden beams. The delicate mesh of the long, brown, funnel-shaped nets had been expertly bated by some of the fishermen and also by the women of the village, before being dressed in the bubbling quayside cauldrons. Then they were laid aboard, triced up aloft by fish tackles to air, the half-inch mesh of the sleeve appearing almost solid, very different from the coarser trawls. The square spars of the upper and lower beams, each some 25 to 30 feet long, were shipped, together with a powerful, long-limbed stowboat anchor. This anchor had to hold both net and vessel against strong tides, wind and sea, the net riding to it, mouth to tide, under the smack's bottom and away astern, by a leg of cable made fast to the lower beam. The lower beam was ballasted with iron to steady the net's mouth, while the upper was held horizontally above it by the templines, ropes which, made fast to the beams ends, passed up to belay on either side of the smacks forward rail. When the net was streamed and fishing its mouth might be 25 to 30 feet square. It was closed by the winch-chain, which started from the lower beam and passed through a ring on the upper one, over a sheave at the end of the stow-davit, fitted in winter on the opposite side of the stem to the gammon iron, and around the windlass barrel. To recover the net this chain was hauled in, bringing the two beams together and to the surface, where the net's sleeve was griped in with ropes, brought on board and its contents emptied into the hold.

It was a fishing gear dating back to the middle ages, and because of the comparatively shoal channels and heavy shipping traffic of the Essex and Kent coasts it was used by the Essex fishermen in preference to the drift nets used elsewhere. Traditionally from about mid-November until about mid-February the stowboat smacks worked their nets by day or night, as the tides served. The skippers watched for the paths of the great sprat shoals, their experience guided by the chase of flocks of gulls. Once located, they let go the anchor down tide and waited for the net to do its work. Sometimes it took a couple of days to get a good haul, which was reckoned as 300 to 400 bushels for a 15 ton smack, though the big Brightlingsea *Masonic* once landed 3000 bushels in a week. Sometimes days or even weeks passed without a worthwhile landing and during that time the fishermen earned nothing; in those days there were no unemployment benefits. It was a fickle living, and all depended on the movements of the shoals. The Wallet and Swin channels were the usual spratting grounds, with Shoe Hole on the Maplins' edge a favourite area. Sometimes the spratting fleet would work the Kentish shore and at others the various channels between the Thames estuary sands, where near the shipping lanes they were sometimes run down and sunk in fog or darkness. Occasionally hauls were made "down the Sunk" and in the Whittaker Channel, and an exceptional schooling of the shoals would lead them to fish in the rivers themselves; under the Blackwater's Bradwell shore or in Colliers Reach, though this was not unusual in the river Orwell. Besides the 12 to 18 tonners, many of the larger smacks, which were becoming fewer by 1900, regularly worked the winter sprat fishery.

In rough weather the stowboaters dreaded a full net. This sometimes happened very suddenly, and the net would float only as long as there was life in the fish. Then the crew wasted no time in getting the net alongside, for if it sank they might never raise it again without damage. Often a full net had to be parted at the lacings to start the fish out of it, enabling the smacksmen to save the net and most of the catch by bailing out a proportion of the catch.

In winter Brightlingsea revolved around spratting: its chances and gluts often eclipsed the oyster trade, which nevertheless remained staple. The little silver fish occupied the town's merchants and curers, the stowboaters' skippers and hands. Brightlingsea, handling half the east coast landings, was the centre of the industry and barometer of its fickle rewards. If prices were low there, smacks from other villages usually sailed their catches to their home port to sell it off as field manure, though prime sprats were landed and cured at other places. Occasionally the larger smacks landed at Chatham or, if prices were good, at Billingsgate Market in London. Often three worked in partnership, each acting as a runner smack in turn, to land the combined catch. Much of Brightlingsea's landings were pickled in barrels with salt, bay leaves and spices, for export to many continental countries, to Russia and to Scandinavia. Much prime fish was smoked by the curers, and some skippers also smoked their own in tall wooden smokehouses. Big landings glutted the market and prices fell rapidly. Then all the skill was to no avail; large the catch and prime the fish might be, yet the hard-won bushel plunged from shillings to mere pence in a few hours. Often the price was fourpence a bushel for manure, the smacks discharging alongside quays piled high with gleaming heaps of unwanted silver sprats.

Traditionally fish-trawling was a short, seasonal fishery for the Colne and Blackwater. Many smacks trawled for roker and soles in the spring and roker and dabs in the autumn, at each end of the spratting season, with occasional winter trawling of offshore codling. Trawling was an ancient tradition in Essex. In 1377 fishermen from the Colne and Blackwater villages were using primitive trawls called *wonderthons* and were causing damage by overfishing, and trawl heads are mentioned in the Ipswich court rolls for 1566. The beam trawl has long been superseded by the otter type but suited the slow speed of sail. The length of beam was determined by the distance from the after shroud to the counter. Most Colne and Tollesbury smacks of about 18 tons and upwards had a double-handed iron capstan amidships which worked the trawl warps. Older smacks often had a wooden capstan with deck treads on which the crew walked, pushing the bars. Recovery of the trawl was aided by the "fish tackle", a purchase leading from the hounds which when required could also serve as a backstay in strong winds and a seaway. Smacks needed two or at the most three hands when trawling, and the proceeds of the catch, as in most Essex fishing, was divided into shares.

After the eighteen-sixties, though most Colne and later Tollesbury smacks laid up for the summer while their crews were yachting, a few carried on with shrimping, which needed only two men to haul the fine-mesh shrimp beam trawl and to riddle, sort and boil the catch on board in a copper installed in the hold. Besides the Essex coastal grounds, some Colne shrimpers also worked out of Grimsby in summer. Other occasional fisheries for the Essex smacks were dredging five-fingers and mussels for field manure or young oysters for re-laying on the grounds of various companies and owners. Seines and peter nets were used to catch mullet by the little transom-sterned Maldon smacks, which also regularly trawled eels on the grassy Mersea Flats or in Suffolk rivers, in company with a dozen or so Merseamen, before 1914. Some of the Mersea smacks also worked for eels in the river Stour and elsewhere. John Howard, the clever Maldon designer and builder of wooden sailing craft, built many of the Maldon transom-sterned smacks, the majority of which had counters built on after 1919 to add deck space for dredging oysters in the river.

The earliest recorded Essex smack races were sailed on the Blackwater in 1783, and by the eighteen-seventies the Colne village regattas had become established annual functions in autumn, when the yachts had laid up and their crews had fitted out the smacks. Regattas were also held at Paglesham in the mid-nineteenth century, and the *Illustrated London News* gives an account of the event in 1838. Tollesbury held its first regatta in 1900.

Most notable of all the racers of this era was Captain Lemon Cranfield of Rowhedge and his rakish smack *Neva*, greyhound of the Colne and Blackwater smack races for over thirty years and built from the fabulous prize money he won in the large class of racing yachts when sailing the Fife-built racing cutter *Neva* in 1876–78. At the height of his fame he was one of the greatest yacht racing helmsmen. The smack *Neva* was built by Harris at Rowhedge, who draughted a straight-stemmed hull with a hollow entrance, filling to a slack midship section that melted into a long run and ended in a graceful counter. A limited wetted-surface made her a great boat in light weather, when she ghosted in the faintest air. Her cutter rig set 1,400 square feet, excluding the spinnaker, which was whisked out to windward by a 38 foot boom—a large rig for a 50 foot fishing vessel.

The new smack lived up to her owner's reputation. Between 1877 and 1907 she repeatedly won the smack races at local regattas against stiff competition. Lemon's skill kept her in front; year after year her mastheadsman proudly jammed the traditional gilt cock at the masthead as she roared first across the finishing line and the band struck up, Lemon acknowledging the cheers with his cap and her crew cheering the second and third. She was beaten on a few occasions, but it was rare. The Wivenhoe *Maria* sometimes managed it and the Rowhedge *Wonder* and William Cranfield's *Sunbeam* also just squeaked in before her a few times.

Not that they were easy victories, as the *Neva* was usually pitted against smacks owned by Lemon's five brothers, who were all noted yachtracing captains: William of *Valkyrie II* and *III* and America's Cup fame competed with the smack *Clara* before buying the swift *Sunbeam*, always a close rival to the *Neva*, John sailed the *Lily*, Stephen the *Blanche* and Richard the *Ellen*. Other noted Rowhedge racing smacks were Captain Simon's *Hildegarde*, Captain James Carter's *Wonder* and the little *Xanthe* sailed by another Captain W. Cranfield.

The *Eudioa* and *Violet* were Wivenhoe's fliers, sailed by the Mason family, and John Gunn's *Maria* was another, while Captain Green's *Elise* always sailed a hard race and once fought it out with the *Ellen*, boat for boat over a twenty-two mile course, to finish within six feet of each other. Stephen Redgewell's *Bertha* was Tollesbury's pride and Brightlingsea's *Foxhound*, *Varuna* and *Volante* were amongst the clippers. Typically, Colne smack race starts were off East Mersea Stone and the course was round the Bar, Priory Spit and Wallet Spitway buoys, then up Colne to finish off whichever village was holding the regatta. Surmises are often made on the speed of the smacks of that time and the recorded times in Wivenhoe regatta for 1884 show that the 20⅞ nautical mile course was won by the *Neva* in 2 hours 23 minutes 4 seconds: an average speed of 8¾ knots. *Wonder* finished second, 2 minutes 56 seconds astern and the *Eudioa* 1 minute 30 seconds after her. Sometimes the race was sailed in a gale, when they started with a single reefed mainsail and topmasts housed, but set spinnakers on the runs.

These were the crack smacks before 1914. Their crews handled them with an easy grace born of a lifetime's familiarity, and their racing was of the highest order. To finish first in that company was prized almost as much as winning a Queen's or King's Cup, for you raced against the same helmsmen.

A similar regatta, with smack racing, was also held at Tollesbury in the early years of this century. That of 1909 was typical, organised by a committee of local yacht skippers and other worthies and offering races for small handicap yachts in a handicap class, for dinghies, rowing, sculling and swimming. But smack races were the principal events. There were two classes of smacks that year, the first for smacks over 18 tons, which sailed a 21 mile course in a fine south-west breeze. The handicap was one second per ton per mile. The Tollesbury *Express* (R. Potter), *Bertha* (W. Redgewell) and *My Alice* (Captain F. Stokes) and the Rowhedge *Sunbeam* (Captain W. Cranfield) and *Wonder* (Captain J. Carter) entered. The presence of the two Rowhedge fliers raised the excitement at this event and they competed annually for two or three years. The Rowhedge *Sunbeam* won the cup and a prize of £8, sailing the 21 mile course in 3 hours, 59 minutes and 37 seconds. The Tollesbury *Express* was second, 6 minutes 8 seconds later, and the *Bertha* third, a further 4 minutes 54 seconds astern. The second class sailed a 14 mile course and this was won by the *M.R.T.* (J. Townsend), with the *Emme* (A. Harris) second and the *Emma Amelia* (S. Lewis) third.

At the Brightlingsea regatta a few days later 13 smacks started in two classes. Although the fisheries under sail were in decline, there was some spirited racing in the Colne and Blackwater in the years before 1914.

Such racing revived during the early nineteen-twenties, but died rapidly with the slump in fishing and the general introduction of auxiliary power into even the fast smacks, to enable a meagre winter living to be earned. However, there has been a vigorous amateur revival since 1946, with smack yachts racing annually at West Mersea Town Regatta, at times also at the Rowhedge and Wivenhoe Regattas, at Brightlingsea, Tollesbury and Maldon. All these events are keenly contested and attract considerable interest.

Since 1900 Essex smacks have occasionally been converted to yachts by admirers of the type and this increased after the decline of sail in the nineteen-thirties. They often needed considerable and costly rebuilding; naturally only the smaller smacks have survived in this way. A few remains of the old first-class smacks still lie rotting in the creeks. But even a small cutter smack is heavy work for amateurs, and most of the smack yachts do not carry topmast, which is a pity, as a topsail is ideal for light weather and generally restores their traditional appearance. The surviving estuary dredgers may lack the tall sparred grace of the larger smacks, but all east coasters are indebted to enthusiasts who preserve and rebuild the old smacks to keep them sailing, for the final passing of their canvas from the estuary and the passing of the regattas will sever a tradition of fishing and racing under sail reaching deep into the past of the Colne and Blackwater seamen.

Oystermen of the Crouch and Roach

Overleaf: Fig. 46. The oyster watchman. Martin Hawes of Burnham on Crouch, sits on the cabin hatch of the watch smack in New England Creek, July, 1914, a few days before the outbreak of the First World War. His bowler hat, incongruous with the blue guernsey, emphasises the difference between the fishermen of the Crouch and Roach and those from the Colne and Blackwater, who adopted a more seafaring appearance. The smack was one of the larger size Burnham cutters and lay at anchor for this duty with the bowsprit run in. It can be seen above his shoulder. The sail, boom and gaff were put ashore for the period of service as a watch smack.
Watch smacks were used at many east coast oyster fisheries in the Crouch, Roach, Blackwater and Medway rivers. Sailing police boats were latterly used in the river Colne. The watchmen on board the moored smack had little power except observation, but that was usually sufficient in conjunction with contemporary laws and judgments.

Above: Fig. 47. The Burnham oyster smack *I.O.P.M.* legged-up to the hard in September 1889. This photograph is of unusual interest as it is of a smack probably built at the end of the eighteenth century or at the beginning of the nineteenth. She has the raking stem and deep fore-gripe, the full body and short lute stern (an early form of counter) of the smacks of that time. The hull has greater depth for her length than many later smacks and the rudder is narrow. The mast is stepped well aft and an iron windlass, set in wooden bitts, appears to be fitted. An estimate of her dimensions, scaling from features shown is that she was probably 35 feet long by 11 feet beam and 7 feet depth from deck at side to bottom of keel. The hull form may be compared with that of the smaller, transom-sterned smack *Boadicea*, built at Maldon in 1809 (fig. 74), and to some extent with the plans of government cutters built in the early nineteenth century.

Above: Fig. 48.   An assortment of craft at Burnham around 1895. In the left foreground is what appears to be one of the large ferry boats used between Burnham and Wallasea Island, on the south bank of the River Crouch. These were often rowed but were sometimes sailed with a large dipping lug or a squaresail. The wooden crutches or rowlocks are interesting and unusual in Essex.

The craft legged-up on the hard foreshore are described from left. First, a full-bodied smack, a steam paddle oyster dredger, one of three or four owned at Burnham. She has her port paddlewheel unshipped. She was tiller steered and had a beamy and full-sectioned hull which was probably built of wood. Beyond her is a small cutter yacht, then a yawl-rigged yacht, while further on is what may be a small oyster dredging cutter converted to a yacht.

The buildings are the sail loft of Nethercoat and the old clubhouse of the Burnham Sailing Club with its bridge.

Overleaf, bottom: Fig. 49. Two small smacks racing in Burnham regatta in 1895. The *Valkyrie* (left) was built that year by John James of Brightlingsea. The *Kate* (right) is of similar size and both are typical of the small smacks that worked the extensive oyster layings in the rivers Crouch and Roach. The tradition of smack racing was established on these rivers by the mid-nineteenth century and possibly before. However, it does not seem to have been as continuous as on the Colne and Blackwater.

Left: Fig. 50. The watch smack for the oyster fishery moored in New England Creek at low water, July, 1914. The lady on deck is the wife of the late Hugh Cohen, an East Coast yachtsman who took these photos. Note the smack's bold sheer and upswept counter. New England Creek was one of several channels between the River Roach and Havengore, an outlet on the Essex shore at the north of the mouth of the Thames, from which a gutway led to the deep water of the estuary. These narrow but surprisingly deep channels were much used by sailing barges and to a lesser extent by fishermen and yachtsmen. About 1920 New England Creek was dammed at the Roach end and it has since been impossible to sail where this photograph was taken.

Right: Fig. 51. Oysters have always attracted theft, and these two broadsheets cautioned oyster dredgers about the claimed rights of the layings owned by the Mildmay family in the River Crouch. The first is dated 1789 and the second 1806. Several forays were made into the Crouch by smacks from the River Colne to dredge oysters. Sometimes they came in numbers and there were several notable tussles. During one of these in March, 1807 between thirty and forty smacks from Rowhedge and Wivenhoe sailed up the River Crouch and started dredging oysters, led by the smack *Betsey* owned by John Willett of Rowhedge. She was boarded by the local customs official, who had the owner and two men taken from her for trial, leaving only the smack's boy on board. The other Colne fishermen gathered angrily and planned to rescue the prisoners but they were hustled ashore and were sentenced quickly by two magistrates to be jailed for theft.

In January, 1808 another raid by Colne smacks occurred and led to a fight and the imprisonment of seven of the smacks' crews. Still undeterred a fleet of thirty-five smacks sailed from Rowhedge, Wivenhoe and Brightlingsea a week later. This was to be the biggest raid, by very determined men, but they were expected and the leaders were arrested. Worse, when the fleet made sail for home the Naval gun brig *Turbulent* was waiting in the lower part of the Crouch and intercepted the fleet, taking several men out of the smacks for naval service. However, at least one smacksman had the last laugh over the Navy. Abraham Lufkin of Rowhedge sued them successfully for wrongful arrest and detention and got £150 in damages, which raised a few chuckles in the Colne and left some red faces on the *Turbulent*.

100

A Caution to Oyster Dredgers.

WHEREAS DAME ANN MILDMAY, the *Widow* and *Relict* of Sir WILLIAM MILDMAY, Bart. is the lawful Owner of a feparate FISHERY in the Waters and Streams called *Burnham River*, otherwife *Wallfleet*, extending from the Weft End, of a certain Place in the faid River, called or known by the Name of *Clay Clods*, down to another Place called or known by the Name of *Ray Sand Head*, and on the *Ray Sand* in the main Sea, in the County of Effex; And her Ladyfhip having received undoubted Information, that many diforderly Perfons have given out, and threatned, that they will enter into the faid feparate Fifhery, and dredge for Oyfters, and alfo enter upon the Oyfter-beds in or near the faid Fifhery, and take away the Oyfters there found, being the fole Property of her Tenants or Leffees:

Notice is Hereby Given,

That her Ladyfhip, on behalf of herfelf, and of her Tenants or Leffees, is determined to Profecute with the utmoft feverity of Law, all Perfons whatfoever who fhall enter into the faid feparate Fifhery, or any of the Waters, or Streams thereunto belonging, and dredge ... or take and carry away any of the Oyfters, or Brood of Oyfters ... or that fhall enter upon the Oyfter-beds, in or near the ... ... ake, fpoil, or deftroy the faid Oyfter-beds, or any of ... the Oyfters therein.

Dated the 27th Day of June, 1789.

CHELMSFORD: Printed by W. Cl...

CAUTION TO OYSTER DREDGERS.

WHEREAS Information having been received by Meffrs. Hawkins and Co. of Burnham, Oyfter Dredgers, who occupy under Sir Henry Mildmay, Bart. and Dame Jane his Wife, the FISHERY in the River called BURNHAM RIVER, otherwife WALL FLEET, extending from the Weft End of a certain Place there called CLAY-CLODS, to a Place called RAY SAND HEAD, and on the RAY-SAND, in the Main Sea, that an UNLAWFUL COMBINATION has been entered into by feveral Oyfter Dredgers in and near Brightlingfea, for the Purpofe of coming into the faid Fifhery, in a large Body, and by Force, dredging for Oyfters therein, and carrying away the fame, the Property of the faid Hawkins and Co.

Notice is hereby given,

That the faid Fifhery is the undoubted Private Property of the faid Sir H. Mildmay, and Dame Jane his Wife; and that the fame hath been enjoyed by them and their Anceftors, without Interruption, from the Time of King Edward the Firft, by whom it was granted; and that all Perfons who fhall come into the faid Fifhery, and dredge therein for Oyfters, will be guilty of a MISDEMEANOUR, and will be punifhable by Law accordingly. And if any Perfon or Perfons, in a Body, or individually, fhall, without Authority, attempt to dredge in the faid Fifhery for Oyfters, he or they will be profecuted for the fame with the utmoft Rigour of the Law.

Dated 16th June, 1806.

MEGGY, CHALK, AND CO. CHELMSFORD.

101

Maldon

Fig. 53. Pole-masted but fully-rigged Maldon smacks line the Hythe in 1939 with booms swung out to list them in on the hard. A couple of gun punts lie to the right and are typical of the undecked Blackwater wildfowling punts. These were sometimes carried on the deck of a smack for a winter wildfowling expedition, enjoyed by Maldon men.

Left: Fig. 52. The small and still very isolated village of Paglesham, on the River Roach, was a considerable centre of oyster cultivation for many years and produced many oyster merchants and dredgermen employed by them. Here a group of Paglesham dredgermen poses outside the Plough and Sail public house about 1910. They were employees of merchants Wiseman, Pettitt and Nicholls. From left to right their names are John Keeble, Walter Fletcher, Jonathan Smith, Alfred Kemp, George Fletcher, James Smith, George Keeble, Fred Alexander, Arthur Smith, George Raisin, Chris Potton and Fred Staines.

At the time the photograph was taken Alfred Kemp was foreman for Nicholls. He and Chris Potton had been rivals for the job and settled it by running a race across the mud!

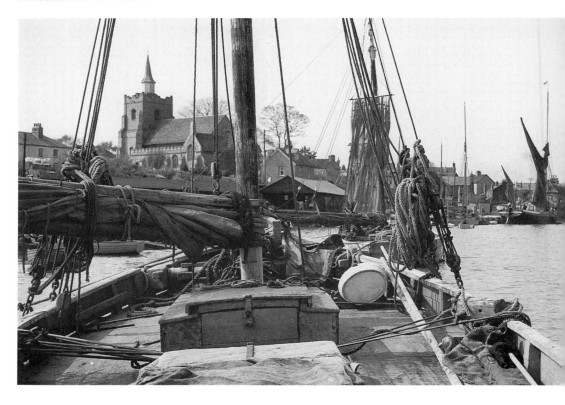

Fig. 54. Sailing smacks and a mill barge drowse in the sunlight of a summer afternoon's high water during 1952.

The little Maldon smacks were mostly fitted with old car engines as auxiliaries by the nineteen-fifties, but retained and used full working rig of mainsail, staysail and a jib, particularly in their staple occupation of dredging oysters in the River Blackwater. The deck of the cutter in the foreground shows typical clutter: a wire oyster basket, the deck bucket, dredges humped over the bulwark rail with the net and wire mesh bottoms hanging down overside and the bass warps coiled on top, a stone water bottle, and some old sacking bags, which had many uses aboard these craft, from working aprons for the crew to carriage of oysters, or preservation of them when hung overboard on a line. The grit-scoured decks and well-worn cabin hatch speak of years of use, but the stowed mainsail is of relatively new and as yet untanned canvas. Despite their continuing use of sail the Maldon fishermen were not nautically minded, sometimes referring to setting a sail at "the back of the mast", and similar solecisms.

The second smack beyond has a peter net hung to dry on a horizontal stave. The Saxon church of St Mary's dominates the quiet waterside and overlooks the sheds of Walter Cook and Sons' bargeyard. One of Green's mill barges is alongside the Town Quay, her topsail and mainsail ready to sail with the ebb for London river and another freight of grain. She is either the *Ethel Maud* or the *Mayflower*. Ahead of her lies the hull of the counter-sterned barge *Mamgu*, then used as a houseboat, usually lying downstream off Osea Island in summer. Built by Gill and Sons of Rochester in 1904 as the *Cawana*, she was owned for many years by R. de B. Crawshay of Heybridge, who also owned the old yawl *Antelope* and the Wivenhoe-built motor cruiser *Beth*.

Fig. 55. Maldon smacks dredging oysters in the Blackwater, about 1955. The transom-sterned smack has a reef in her mainsail and a small jib set to reduce speed for dredging. When oysters were laid in the upper parts of the Blackwater during the mid-nineteenth century many Maldon fishermen complained that the oyster interests would ruin their traditional fisheries trawling for flatfish and eels. In 1892 one old Maldon fisherman commented "There ain't no fish in the river now; not what yew might call fish to make a livin' out of. When that grass growed everywhere in the river, there was plenty of 'em. I've took eight stone of a mornin' before breakfast, hereabouts, when I was a lad along o' my father. But they've got them oysters down and that grass don't grow on the banks like what it used to, not anything like, and the fish ain't nothin' to what they was then. I don't see the good of them oysters to us fishermen. There's two or three o' them gentlemen in Lundon as gets rich by it, and all by the layin' of 'em down on our banks what belonged to us afore ever they was born. The river belongs to us and I reckon the banks do too; an' there'ud be plenty of fishin' in the river now if they was to let that grass grow agen in the river like that used to. Curse them oysters, I says; I don't like 'em and I don't want them neather." In later years the Maldoners derived much work from the river's oysters but the old man's view was probably typical of his contemporaries.

Fig. 56. The Maldon smack *Polly* was one of several built by John Howard at his Maldon yard for the Pitt family in the eighteen-eighties. She was the last smack at Maldon to work without an auxiliary engine, as late as the mid-nineteen-fifties, and sailed well. Like many of the Maldon smacks she was small and was built with a transom stern. A counter was added in 1919 to afford more deck space when oyster dredging became a more frequent part of the Maldon fishermen's work. Previously they had principally been peter-netting, winkling or trawling for bottom fish. The *Polly* was fast for her size and won races against similar-sized smacks at West Mersea and Maldon regattas.

Tollesbury

Fig. 57. The smack *Pride* discharging five-fingers (starfish) at saltings near Copt Hall, Little Wigborough, in the eighteen-nineties. Several smacks from the Colne and from Tollesbury sometimes dredged for five-fingers, landing them in bulk for use as farm manure. Although a poor print, this photograph is the only known one of a smack discharging this cargo. She is in a rill of the great marsh that sweeps from Tollesbury, through an arc behind Mersea Island to the river Colne in the east.

Fig. 58. The Tollesbury smack *Daisy*, CK 6, in light airs. She appears to be towing two yacht's boats, perhaps to or from a regatta. The shape of her counter was unusual in its steep upward sweep. The quarter boards are shipped on top of the bulwarks aft. These were usually carried in winter to provide some additional protection for the helmsman and for others working aft at ropes and nets. She has one reef in the mainsail. The *Daisy* was at one time owned at Wivenhoe.

Right: Fig. 59. Tollesbury fisherman Harry Myall at the tiller of the family smack *S.W.H.*, named for Sidney, William and Harry Myall. Dress and stance are typical. The photograph was taken in the early years of this century.

Below: Fig. 60. The smack, *Dove*, III CK, owned by J. Pearce of Tollesbury in the Wallet, a Colne-built smack in typical working trim for fish-trawling or shrimping. A photograph taken in 1921.

Above: Fig. 61. Smack MN 29 in the Blackwater, June 1918. She is unusually setting a large light-weather jib and also another set on the staysail halyard with the tack to the bowsprit end. During the 1914–18 war Essex fisheries were at first very restricted, but later the smacks were permitted to work in defined areas and some obtained government contracts for sprats in the years of food shortage from 1916 to 1918. Fishing was restricted to the coastal waters, which were patrolled by motor launches and armed trawlers and drifters that often proved more of a hazard to the fishermen than did any threat of enemy action.

Right: Fig. 62. By the nineteen-forties there were few reminders of the former imposing appearance of the smacks. Rigs were cut down, usually to a light mast on which a staysail could be set with a fresh, fair wind or to steady the hull in a seaway. Here some smacks and motor shrimpers lie at Harwich, about 1947. CK 104 in the foreground is the Tollesbury smack *Bluebell*, owned by L. Heard. A close-meshed shrimp trawl hangs from her mast; she remains tiller steered. At that time very few smacks had a wheelhouse fitted. By the nineteen-fifties new vessels were being built for the Essex fleet, having transom sterns, less draught and wheelhouses. Now they too have largely been superseded by a variety of craft built of steel and GRP and of various sizes and arrangements.

West Mersea

Fig. 63. Two small West Mersea smacks sail out of the Quarters in light weather on a town regatta morning in the nineteen-thirties. Both set large balloon staysails. For some years after the nineteen-twenties smacks racing at West Mersea were allowed only three sails: mainsail, staysail and a jib, though the headsails could be of any desired area. Topsails and spinnakers were not carried, as by then almost all the Mersea and Maldon smacks did not carry a topmast or have a spinnaker in their daily work. Booming out of headsails was not allowed when racing, to limit the area which could be carried. As a result, before the wind, one hand had to stand on the bulwark, by the weather shrouds, and strain an outstretched arm to act as a human boom in an attempt to fill the balloon staysail on the weather side as a spinnaker, a task I have performed several times.

Fig. 64. Tollesbury and Mersea oystermen at the oyster packing shed and pits, West Mersea, about 1913. The group includes: A. Carter, Joe Pearce, Jack Pearce, Isaiah Binks, Nehemiah Ward, A. Rice, John Redgwell, R. Page, William Collins, James Heard, Joseph Heard, Michael Heard, Peter Frost, J. Pettican and several of the Mole family of West Mersea.
Many are wearing sack aprons. Sacks and sacking bags were much used in the oyster trade. The commonest complaint of the oysterman was "Can't niver git enough baigs, boy".

Fig. 65. The West Mersea smack *Charlotte* as a smack-yacht owned by Hervey Benham, racing in the West Mersea Town regatta, about 1938. This shows the beam and broad quarters of these small smacks and the full cut of the mainsail.

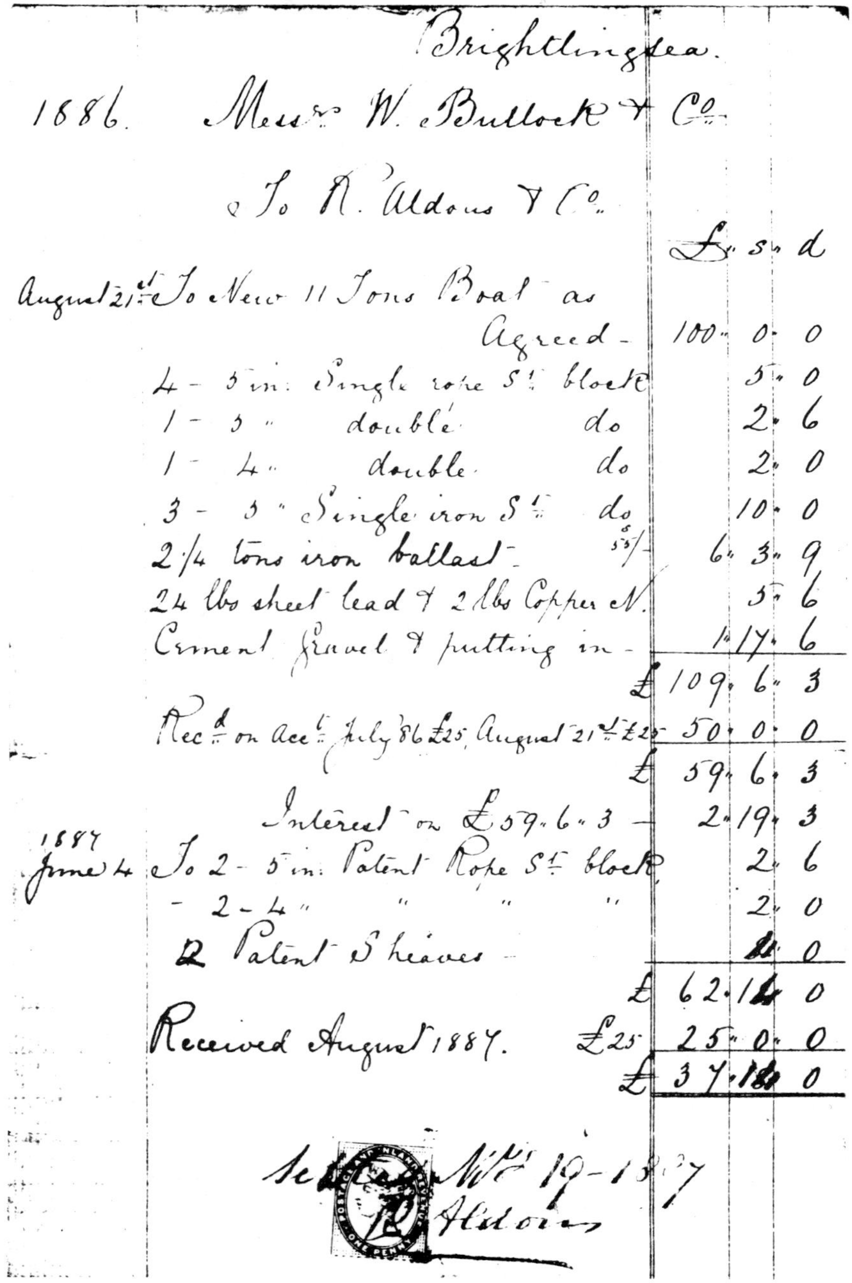

Brightlingsea.

1886.   Messrs W. Bullock & Co.

        To R. Aldous & Co.

	£	s	d
August 21st To New 11 Tons Boat as Agreed	100	0	0
4 - 5 in. Single rope St block		5	0
1 - 5 " double do		2	6
1 - 4 " double do		2	0
3 - 3 " Single iron St do		10	0
2 1/4 tons iron ballast 53/	6	3	9
24 lbs sheet lead & 2 lbs Copper N.		5	6
Cement gravel & putting in	1	17	6
	£109	6	3
Recd on Acct July 86 £25, August 21st £25	50	0	0
	£59	6	3
Interest on £59.6.3	2	19	3
1887 June 4 To 2 - 5 in. Patent Rope St block		2	6
- 2 - 4 " " " "		2	0
2 Patent Sheaves		2	0
	£62	10	0
Received August 1887. £25	25	0	0
	£37	10	0

Stamped Nd 19 - 1887
R Aldous

Fig. 66.   A receipted account for the construction of an 11 ton smack by Robert Aldous and Co. of Brightlingsea for W. Bullock and Co., oyster merchants, 1886. The hull-mast and spars cost £100 but blocks, iron ballast and other outfit items were charged extra. The prices make an interesting contrast with those a century later. The relative stability of costs and prices at the time contributed significantly to the continuation of many long established methods of work and business, including the fisheries.

114

Right: **Fig. 67.** The oysterman George Stoker of West Mersea before the "offoce" of the Stag's Head Oyster Fishery Co. Ltd in the nineteen-forties. The cap, oilskin and thigh boots were typical wear in winter and the sturdy trade bike propped against the shed was an indispensable adjunct to any Mersea oysterman.

Below: **Fig. 68.** An oyster feast on board a large smack on the occasion of the start of a new dredging season on the Blackwater. It is possible that the smack is the 21 ton *Aquiline* of Rowhedge, owned by Captain Harry Cook. At times before 1914 she carried foreign imported oysters in large quantities from the London docks for re-laying on the grounds off Heath.

Above: Fig. 69. Culling oysters for size and quality. The flat basket at left was much used by oystermen, particularly when collecting young oysters on the flats and layings. It was called a tendal, for unknown reasons.

Left: Fig. 70. A full-grown native oyster with opened shell displayed with some of the pests which oystermen are constantly trying to subdue. At bottom left are slipper limpets, and the others are borers.

Above: Fig. 71. A view of the stern of the West Mersea smack *Mary*, owned by the Pullen family. She is the last Essex smack to survive with a lute stern—an early form of counter in which a concave plane of transverse planking curves out from the tuck at the sternpost to deck level. Above this it is carried across at a different angle, for the depth of the bulwark.

Right: Fig. 72. William Wyatt the West Mersea boatbuilder hoists the mainsail of the bumkin *Ma'nabs*. The gaff sloop rig resembled that of a smack in miniature. Such craft made good stable platforms for minor fishing or carrying oysters or shell for laying as culch on oyster layings, or for winkling, either in the river or down on the Main, as working on the Dengie flats was called.

Fig. 73. A very rare photo of West Mersea bumkins, as sailing oyster skiffs and winkling boats were known locally, on the south shore of the island, loading passengers for sailing trips on the Blackwater on a summer's morning in 1920. This pleasant activity continued for several years after the First World War, when few could afford to own a small boat of their own. These well-scrubbed, beamy little open fishing boats were ideal for a sail off the beach at a time of year when trippers were plentiful and fishing was slack.

Fig. 74. West Mersea and Maldon smacks at the start of a race in West Mersea Town Regatta in the nineteen-thirties. The *Boadicea*, on the extreme right, was built at Maldon in 1809. She is still sailing after being rebuilt by the late Michael Frost of Colchester and remains an occasional competitor in the Essex smack races. She is now owned by Mrs Frost.

Rowhedge

Fig. 75. A scale model of the hull of the Rowhedge smack *Sunbeam* CK 328, owned by Captain William W. Cranfield. The lines of this fast smack were accurately taken off by Mr Henry Higgs, who made this model. It shows her well-raked sternpost and rounded forefoot. The *Sunbeam* was typical in dimensions of the many smacks of about 18 tons register owned at Rowhedge, where there were also many larger and some smaller smacks until 1914.

Fig. 76. Colne smacks also dredged oysters on the north Norfolk coast at times and at several other places when further away from Essex waters. Here, CK 97 lies on the hard at Blakeney, Norfolk. Believed to be Jack Spitty's *Thorn*, she was one of many Colne smacks which sailed there to dredge the once profitable beds, which they soon worked out to the despair of the locals. This sad process they were to repeat in many places around Britain and on the coast of France. This photograph was taken about 1890 and shows the shapely hull of this typical Colne smack and particularly the fine entrance of her bow.

119

Fig. 77. Recovering a stowboat net; the crew of the Rowhedge smack *Ellen* CK 321, stowboating in the nineteen-twenties. They are passing girdlines around the sleeve of the stow net and have hauled a forward sleeve up on the masthead tackle to clear it out of the way, the fish having been worked aft from it. The mainsail is stowed and a cloud of gulls hover expectantly. The quarter boards are rigged, as is the binnacle for the compass on the hatch to the cabin, aft. The shroud deadeyes and lanyards are woulded with rope to avoid chafe from the net, and the main ropes are rigged from the shrouds forward to give some protection to those working on the foredeck.

The 50 foot *Ellen* was built at Wivenhoe in 1886 for Walter Leavett, who then owned Rowhedge Ferry. He let her to fishermen to work in winter and to yachting parties in the summer—the only known local instance of such speculation. She was often let to the Glozier family for shrimping in summer, working out of the river Humber in Yorkshire in company with the Wivenhoe smack *Elise* and the Yorkshire cutters from Paull. For summer party sailing a skylight was fitted over the main hatch and berths were erected in the hold. She made several yachting trips to the continent with a Rowhedge crew. Leavett sold her to Zac Burch, who resold her to Captain Richard Cranfield of Rowhedge for about £250, then an average price for such a smack. She paid for herself in eighteen months of good, skilful fishing by that consummate seaman, who was a noted yacht captain.

The *Ellen* was a spectacular performer in the smack race on regatta day, and strangely the *Ellen* and *Elise* once finished within six feet of each other in a Rowhedge Regatta smack race after sailing a 22 mile course, such was the rivalry and spirit and skill of the smacks' skippers and crews, who settled the year's yachtracing scores in those annual tussles. After 40 years with the Rowhedge smack fleet and still a spectacular performer on regatta days, she was sold to Harry Death of Brightlingsea, who fished her from there until the Second World War, when she was hulked.

Fig. 78. Elegance of the Colne smacks. Three Rowhedge smacks racing out of the river Colne in the village regatta, about 1903. From left to right are *Sunbeam* CK 328, Captain William W. Cranfield (noted skipper of racing yachts such as the *Yarana*, *Valkyrie II* and *Valkyrie III*), the *Neva* CK 86, Captain Lemon Cranfield, brother to William and skipper of many noted racers including the schooners *Pantomime* and *Miranda* and the cutters *Britannia*, *Neva*, *Galatea*, *Foxhound* and others. The smack at right is the *Xanthe*, Captain "Bill" Cranfield (who was not related to the others. These three smacks were amongst the fastest from the Colne in the period from the late eighteen-eighties to 1914. The *Neva* and *Sunbeam* were frequent winners of the local smack races, where the honour of finishing first was almost equal to winning a race in the big class yachts of the time. The same men were at the helm and the crews were some of the same men. The rigs were their usual working canvas with yard-topsails set for the light weather. Many smacks carried white sails and these were only tanned when they became discoloured. The *Neva* had less sheer than many of her contemporaries but was very fast. The *Sunbeam* was recently rebuilt and refitted to sailing condition and is now owned at Tollesbury. The *Xanthe* was sold to owners in Wivenhoe and worked under sail into the nineteen-twenties. Later she became a hulk in Alresford Creek and broke up.

Fig. 79. Captain Lemon Cranfield's smack *Neva* 86 CK of Rowhedge, soon after the start of a smack race in the Colne about 1905. She was designed and built by the Harris brothers at Rowhedge and was named after the 60 ton cutter yacht with which Lemon won many races in the eighteen-seventies, part of a brilliant career in yacht racing which left him acknowledged as its genius.
Here the hands forward are sending up a balloon foresail. The mainsail sets badly at the foot and clew. It may have been a new sail, as every care was taken with the cut and set of canvas by these men. The quarterboards are shipped and a lifebelt is placed over the trawl capstan amidships. After Lemon Cranfield's death in 1911 the *Neva* was sold to Brightlingsea owners and is believed to have been owned eventually at Boston in Lincolnshire.

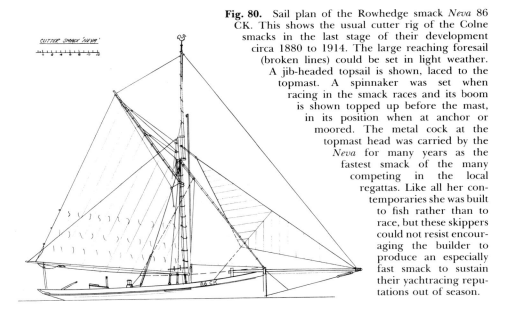

Fig. 80. Sail plan of the Rowhedge smack *Neva* 86 CK. This shows the usual cutter rig of the Colne smacks in the last stage of their development circa 1880 to 1914. The large reaching foresail (broken lines) could be set in light weather. A jib-headed topsail is shown, laced to the topmast. A spinnaker was set when racing in the smack races and its boom is shown topped up before the mast, in its position when at anchor or moored. The metal cock at the topmast head was carried by the *Neva* for many years as the fastest smack of the many competing in the local regattas. Like all her contemporaries she was built to fish rather than to race, but these skippers could not resist encouraging the builder to produce an especially fast smack to sustain their yachtracing reputations out of season.

122

Fig. 81. Regatta day at Row-hedge around 1906. Besides the smacks racing in the village regatta there were others which remained at their usual moorings by the village quays. Here, Jonathan Cranfield's smack *Lily* lies with the deck clear of gear and gang-plank rigged for the owner's family, relatives and friends. A yacht's boat with a village party on board lies alongside and the style of dress afloat and ashore would rival contemporary Henley. "Upstreet" (right) is another smack alongside the quay by the Anchor pub and just beyond her a ketch barge is delivering coal at the Lion Quay for Charles Crosby's coal yard. The big shed of the shipyard is in the background. Except for demolition of the two houses by the ferry hard, this view of Rowhedge waterside has changed only a little.

Fig. 82. Occasionally in summer or autumn a smack might take the owner's family and a few friends for "a day down the river". Here a Wivenhoe smack is fetching upstream in the bight below Wivenhoe in the light airs of an evening tide after just such a day. The ladies of the pleasure party wear the long dresses and ornate best hats of the Edwardian era, even for this short trip afloat. The trawl beam shows to port and the smack's rowboat is being paddled along aft. The topping lift is set up, probably to give some clearance for unwary heads.

Fig. 83. A close finish! Captain Green's *Elise* CK 299 of Wivenhoe (left) and Captain Richard Cranfield's *Ellen* of Rowhedge (right) pass Harris' shipyard, where both were built, to finish within six feet of each other after racing a 22 mile course in Rowhedge regatta, probably about 1921 and one of the last held in the old style.

The Salvagers

Fig. 84. Thomas Barnard of Rowhedge, the author's great-grandfather, photographed on Rowhedge quay in the eighteen-eighties. He was a fisherman, salvager, oyster merchant and occasionally smuggler, owning the smacks *Prince of Orange, Morgan, Racer* and *New Unity*. He typified the adventurous mariners of the Colne, amongst the world's finest fore and aft seamen, fiercely independent and quick as gulls to seize any chance the sea brought. In numerous salvaging and life saving exploits with his smacks he and his crews rescued over 900 people from wrecks and stranded ships, usually in severe conditions. His long life afloat ended with the loss of his last and largest smack, the 33 ton *New Unity*, during a blizzard. He survived to enjoy his retirement at Rowhedge, where his sons and grandsons continued the family seafaring tradition in smacks, yachts and steamships.

124

Fig. 85. Cutter smacks salvaging from a wrecked merchant ship, painted by Henry Redmore (1820–87) in 1872, when such sights were still commonplace on the East Coast. Hundreds of vessels were lost in this way until the last quarter of the nineteenth century, when steamships began to oust the sailing merchantmen and the number of strandings dropped rapidly, becoming rare by the eighteen-nineties.

Redmore has painted powerful looking cutter smacks typical of those sailing from the Essex coast in the mid-nineteenth century. Three of these are sailing around the wreck. The smack at the right is hove to under a full mainsail with its tack triced up and the foresail "backed-over". The smack in the foreground has her topping lift set up and the mainsail tack triced, but the foresail is drawing and she is sailing slowly towards the wrecked ship's stern. In the distance another smack sails a reciprocal course. All are waiting for the sea to moderate so that their boats may board the wreck, perhaps when the tide turns. As far as is known this is an imaginary incident, but it is entirely typical of the thousands which occurred along the east coast and particularly on the myriad shoals off the coast of Essex and the approach to the Thames.

Fig. 86. One of the most horrific wrecks on the Essex coast was that of the North German Lloyd liner *Deutschland* on the Kentish Knock sand in December, 1875. She struck in a north-easterly gale and fifty-seven people were swept from her before the boats from salvaging smacks could reach her in the violent conditions. Cargo, fittings, spars and equipment were salvaged from her afterwards, as was customary. This was supposed to be landed at the depot of the receiver of wrecks, usually at Brightlingsea or Harwich, when a proportion of the value was paid to the smack owners for division among their crews; at times there were unauthorised runs made with some of the spoils. The whole business of salvaging on the Essex coast and elsewhere was a mixture of heroism in saving lives, of hard and often dangerous work in salvaging from the wreck, and finally and frequently acrimonious exchanges in a court, where the salvagers' claims were settled often to their dissatisfaction.

Wivenhoe

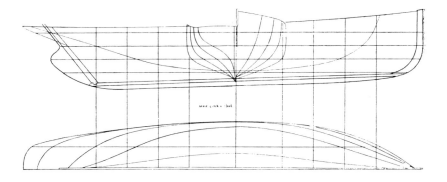

Above: Fig. 87.   The smack *Elise* CK 299, owned by Captain Green of Wivenhoe, with a party of the owner's family and friends on board for a day's fishing. The *Elise* is slipping along under working sails, including a balloon foresail and big jib, to suit the light airs of an autumn morning. The topsail has a short yard at its head and stands well. The anchor is being carried at the bow instead of being catted up with a lashing at the sheer, as was more usual. This was to allow it to be let go quickly again if she was totally becalmed.

The *Elise* was designed and built by Enos and Peter Harris at Rowhedge in the eighteen-eighties. She was typical of the Colne smacks of that time, built for spratting and fish-trawling, but also capable of dredging shellfish or shrimp-trawling if necessary. The Green family has a long association with fishing and remains active in the trade, with retail shops and a motor fishing vessel.

Opposite: Fig. 88.   Lines of a Colne smack built around 1870. This shows the typical hull form of the Colne fishing smacks of between 15 and 18 tons, which were a size much used during the latter half of the nineteenth century as a useful general purpose craft capable of fishing in rough conditions and of making passages around the British coasts and to continental waters. The rig was a cutter with a topsail, and these smacks were in general fast sailers. They were used for spratting with a stow net, for trawling, salvaging from wrecks and for dredging oysters, scallops and five-fingers (starfish) in various localities on the east, south and west coasts of England, in the North Sea, the English Channel, Scotland, and off the coasts of Holland and France. The hull is fairly full bodied and has a moderate rise of floor to give a good carrying capacity of a load of sprats or other fish. The deep forefoot and straight keel made these craft steady on the helm for fishing, particularly when trawling and dredging, and the forward sheer enabled them to stand hard driving to windward, though the comparatively low after freeboard made many wet in bad weather, which they and their crews withstood magnificently.

127

Fig. 89. Colne smacks racing, about 1907. In the foreground is the Wivenhoe *Elise*, Captain Green, which was often successful in the village regattas and equally so in the fisheries. Beyond is the *Maria*, Mr Gunn of Wivenhoe, and then the *Sunbeam* of Rowhedge, Captain W. W. Cranfield. In this race a stipulation was made that the smacks were to sail with a beam trawl on deck, an unusual requirement, and it is not now known why this handicap was imposed. The wave-making qualities of the hulls, here sailing at speed, is interesting, particularly if one studies the wake of the *Elise*. The mainsail of the *Elise* shows three rows of reef points, with the earing of the first reef rove and hanging below the boom. The variety of topsails was typical, each being chosen according to the particular skipper's thoughts on what was most efficient in the prevailing conditions.

Fig. 90. An oystering idyll. Three generations of the Bartlett family of Wivenhoe on board their small smack *Diamond* after dredging in the Geeton Creek of the river Colne, about 1905. Here is all the clutter indispensable for river oystering under sail. The chain-mesh bottoms of the dredges are visible amidships, by the bulwark, where a tendal basket lies with some oysters spilling from it. Dredge warps are coiled about the deck and a pair of large sweeps are in the foreground and have probably been used to get the little smack down to the layings on this fine, calm day. The elder Bartletts wear leather sea boots, and on this warm morning the younger man sports a canvas sun hat from his service on yachts. The white flax mainsail hangs idly and the atmosphere is one of peace.

Brightlingsea

Fig. 91. Robert Aldous, the Brightlingsea ship, yacht, smack and boat builder (centre with white beard) inspecting work in his yard with his foreman and later partner Robert Rashbrook (left, in bowler hat, on gangway). The forms of the laid-up yachts in the background suggests the late eighteen-nineties as the date of this photograph. Large numbers of smacks and bawleys were built in this yard besides many other craft. Later, it became a steel shipyard under the title of Aldous Successors Ltd but continued to build wooden craft. It closed in 1963. The site is now occupied by a commercial wharf and by small firms, some building yachts and small boats.

Fig. 92. Numbers of smacks laid up at Underwood's Hard in Brightlingsea Creek during the summer yachting season, when their crews were away as skippers and hands in yachts of all types and sizes, particularly the racing classes, in which the Colne men excelled. This division of the year into winter fishing and summer yachting was the way of life for most mariners from Brightlingsea, Wivenhoe and Rowhedge for over a century, with others from Tollesbury and West Mersea joining in after the eighteen-nineties until 1939. Experience in yachts and a natural quest for speed led to the refinement of smack form, rig and handling, particularly during the period between, roughly, 1850 and 1890, when many local smacks were built.

Fig. 93. Smacks fitting out on Brightlingsea Hard in November, 1934. By the nineteen-twenties engines were fitted in most of the Colne smacks, and when this photograph was taken the numbers of smacks owned in the Colne was declining. The larger smack in the centre is the *Masonic*, a typical Colne cutter smack. Her quarter boards are rigged for the winter fisheries, but the rudder is temporarily unshipped for repairs. The flat and shallow counter of the smack at the extreme right of the photograph is unusual.

Brightlingsea hard was for many years the centre of activity for the local smack fleet. The wide hard was made up during the eighteen-nineties by a local benefactor, who stipulated it remain free for all time to the fishermen of Brightlingsea.

Fig. 94. An oyster dredging smack lying alongside the steam paddle dredger *Pyefleet* while the crew cull oysters on deck. This photograph was taken about 1905. The fishery foreman and another compare tallies in the beamy oyster skiff loaded with sacks of oysters and laying outside the smack.

These skiffs were often 18 to 22 feet long and with about 8 feet beam, clinker planked and built with strong oak-sawn frames fitted over the lands of the English elm planking. Stout floors of fir stiffened the bottom for laying on hard ground with a load of oysters or with culch or shram for preparing the layings. Skiffs were usually sculled with an oar over the stern, and with a fair tide or in slack water could make good progress.

Fig. 95. Oystermen of the Colne Fishery Company cleaning and sorting oysters in the shed on Peewit Island, in the Pyefleet Creek off the river Colne, 1949. From left to right are H. Death, A. French, F. Everett, F. Ellis and the fishery foreman, G. Francis. All were from Brightlingsea and represented the last generation of the old style oystermen, fishermen and yacht hands to work the river into the nineteen-fifties.

Fig. 96. Two smacks lying on Brightlingsea Hard for a scrub, about 1928. The cutter to the left has her mainsail set with two reefs taken in. The quarter boards are shipped. She appears to have a pole mast and has almost certainly been fitted with an auxiliary engine but retains her rig of mainsail, Staysail and jib. The other smack is slightly smaller and has a trawl hoisted for drying. The Anchor Hotel is to the right and the sheds of J. James and Co., yacht-builders, are to the left.

FISHING BOATS LYING ON THE HARD
BRIGHTLINGSEA

131

Left, top: Fig. 97.   Unique photo of a large Colne cutter smack under sail. The Brightlingsea smack *Globe* CK 73 photographed entering Newhaven in Sussex after dredging scallops in the English Channel. Her crew of five are on deck and her boat is carried on the starboard quarter, canted against the bulwarks. Her counter stern rises at a steeper angle than in many smacks and reflects her date of building. Altogether the *Globe* was typical of the Colne first-class smacks of about 60 feet length.

Newhaven was a frequent place of refuge in bad weather for the Colne smacks working in the English Channel at different fishing seasons and it was also much used to land Channel-dredged oysters and scallops, which were sent to Billingsgate, London's fishmarket, by rail. The *Globe* was owned by Captain Jabez Polley of Brightlingsea and was built at Wivenhoe in 1805.

Left, bottom: Fig. 98.   Four large cutter smacks, including Essex vessels from the Colne, lying in Newhaven harbour, Sussex, in the eighteen-nineties while dredging oysters and scallops in the English Channel. The white sails were typical of those of many smacks. Usually their sails were not dressed with a coloured preservative, such as cutch, until they were worn and badly stained with mildew, against which these craft are airing their canvas.

Overleaf: Fig. 99. The Brightlingsea first-class smack *Hilda* in Mounts Bay, Cornwall, on passage down Channel to fishing grounds on the west coast. The 40 ton *Hilda* was built at Brightlingsea in 1886 as a cutter, but was later converted to ketch rig. This 65-footer engaged in many of the fisheries that were worked by the Colne smacks, from spratting to dredging oysters and scallops in the North Sea and English Channel, on the West Coast and in the Solway Firth. For many years she was under the managing ownership of William Holland and was fishing until 1935.

Above: Fig. 100. William Francis of Brightlingsea, foreman of the Colne Fishery Company, at the helm of the Company smack *Native* in 1928. He typified the smacksman, as accustomed to facing a North Sea gale as to dredging oysters in a quiet creek. They were usually quiet, resourceful men, spending their summers as crew in racing, cruising, steam or motor yachts and their winters fishing under sail in smacks large and small. Rubber thigh boots had replaced the greased leather sea boots with wooden-pegged soles of earlier times, but the guernsey and cheesecutter cap remained and with the toil-stained trousers and "wesket" complete a portrait of a seaman at work in a well-mastered environment. The cluttered deck was typical of a dredging smack sailing up-tide to prepare for another haul with the dredges: an apparent tangle of bass warps, iron dredge frames, chain-mesh dredge bottoms and netting backs, a sweep and all the gear of a sailing smack.
The reef earings are rove for the first and second reefs; the first led to the reef tackle purchase along the boom. A bass mainsheet was used because it wore well in this work, was inexpensive and had plenty of spring in it for gybing and manoeuvring in strong winds: a tradition carried over from the big North Sea smacks. The light lines seized around the booms are for stowing the mainsails but add to the apparently unkempt appearance of these small smacks.
The *Native* was unusual for a Colne smack in having been built with a transom stern for the Colne Fishery Company. The hull form was subtle and pleasing. The *Claude* was similar. Almost all others had counters like 133 CK sliding past astern, a typical small smack of the type used for oyster dredging and fish trawling in the estuary of the Colne and Blackwater rivers and the adjacent coastal waters. She would perhaps have ventured occasionally on a longer trip, though she is a little small in length, freeboard and hull capacity for stowboating. Her cutter rig is typical but the much patched light-weather jib and light canvas of her sails mark her present work as dredging in sheltered waters. The high-cut foot of the mainsail is unusual and the forestay connects to the stem head by a deadeye, with lanyards spread through holes bored transversely through the stemhead. She cuts along well, with the foresail just lifting and her crew in attitudes of ease as she sails to the next haul.

Fig. 101. Repairing a sprat net on the deck of a smack in Brightlingsea Creek, 1937. Here part of the huge net is flaked over the stowed mainsail to repair small rents, possibly caused when raising it when full on the preceding trip. The fishermen wear the mixture of clothing usual at the time: cloth caps contrasting with blue guernseys, pilot-cloth jackets and trousers from their yachting outfits. One man wears an *Endeavour* guernsey. The decks of the smacks in the background are cluttered with stowboat baulks and nets.

Sprats were one of the main winter fisheries of the Essex coast, and thousands of tons of these small silver fish were landed in a few months, usually from mid November to mid February. Most of this harvest was sold very cheaply to local farmers for field fertiliser. Much of the Brightlingsea landings was pickled in barrels with bay leaves, salt and spices for export to Germany, Russia, Holland and Norway. A good deal of prime fish was smoked by the curers and some skippers also smoked their own in small wooden smokehouses set on the quays or in their gardens.

The stow net was made up of several parts, and its mouth was spread by upper and lower baulks about 26 feet long. When fishing for sprats the smack lay to a heavy stowboat anchor and a long scope of cable, usually but not always chain. Often the chain was moulded around a strong bass rope to give a resilient cable. The smack rode to the anchor head to tide, with the lower baulk connected to the cable and with ballast to make it sink. The upper baulk was held square above it with ropes called templines leading from its ends to belay on either bow of the smack. So, in use, the mouth of the net was usually about 26 feet square. It was closed by a "winchain", which lifted the lower baulk upwards to join the upper baulk, at which it passed through a ring, then over the baulk davit at the stem head and to the barrel of the windlass, which was used to raise it. When the net was at the surface it was brought alongside with ropes and the sprats were got on deck.

continued The stowboating smacks might fish day or night to suit the tides, the quality of daylight at dusk or dawn, on grounds and locations from the North Foreland to the Suffolk coast, though the Swin and the Wallet were favoured places for sprats. The skippers were guided by seabirds feeding on the sprat shoals, local water discoloration and other signs, coupled with their experience and intuition.

Smacks set their gear downtide of the expected shoals and waited for fish in bulk to enter the net. It might take a few hours or more than a day to gather a worthwhile catch. A 50-foot smack might be lucky and land 300 to 400 bushels, but there were periods when days and sometimes weeks went by without a catch, and during that time the fishermen had to support themselves from savings, usually from the income from summer yachting.

Fig. 102. First-class Colne smacks from Rowhedge and Brightlingsea lying in harbour at Isle of Whithorn, on the Solway Firth, Scotland, in the eighteen-eighties. A fleet of fifty or so sailed there to dredge oysters in Luce Bay, making their passage down Channel and around Land's End. These 65 to 70 foot cutters were powerful vessels, and in such craft the Colne fishermen voyaged to oyster and scallop grounds around the British coasts and to grounds off the coasts of Holland, France and the Channel Islands. They found grounds off the Dudgeon, near the Norfolk coast, near Newhaven in the Firth of Forth, Largo Bay on the Fife coast, the Straits area of North Wales, at Falmouth, in the eastern part of the English Channel, around Cap d'Ailly and other parts of the French coast and off the Dutch island of Terschelling, as well as in other places.

The smack in the centre of the picture, CK 142, is a typical example of the larger Colne smacks and has the fine lines of the type. The rig had a generous area and the topmast was well sprung forward to counteract the pull of the mainsail and topsail when set. She sits on legs shipped under the shroud channels. Her boat lies before her. It is typically sizable for carrying a number of men, fishing gear and stores to and from the smack, often in exposed waters and for salvage work. It would be carried on deck when on passage.

CHAPTER SEVEN

Harwich

THE OLD seafaring town of Harwich, at the confluence of the rivers Orwell and Stour, on the border of Essex and Suffolk, had fishing interests going back through the centuries to the search for cod as far away as Iceland. Besides the fleet of cod smacks, which survived into the early twentieth century, Harwich, like Leigh, became aware of the possibilities of the shrimp trade. It was carried on from Harwich by smacks and by bawleys that were identical with those of Leigh. About sixty bawleys fished from Harwich in the heyday before 1914. Most of these were owned by members of the Good, Denny and Smith families. Between May and September they were shrimp-trawling off Walton and Clacton, in the Wallet Channel, inside the Gunfleet Sand, off Felixstowe in Suffolk and around the Cork and the Cutler shoals. From September until May the whelking season found them working off the Ridge near Harwich and under the Pye sands.

Besides trawling for shrimps, there were in 1900 about twenty bawleys and small smacks fishing all year round from Harwich for whelks, which were used as bait for long-line fishing by large smacks owned at Harwich and elsewhere. This trade declined considerably after 1914 but a reduced demand remained for the summer seaside trade. Some Harwich bawleys were laid up in winter, when topmasts were sent down and sails and gear laid ashore in store until the spring.

Many of the Harwich bawleys were built at the port and others were constructed there for Leigh and proved fast and able craft. Several notably fast bawleys were built at Harwich by George Cann and later his sons John and Herbert, whose firm of J. and H. Cann closed in 1922. George Cann was apprenticed at Aldous' shipyard at Brightlingsea and worked there afterwards as a shipwright before leaving to start his own yard at Harwich in about 1868. This was situated at the head of Gasworks Creek and the firm was at first known as Parsons and Cann, though nothing is known of Parsons. George Cann built himself a house opposite the yard and settled down to build and repair wooden craft. Sailing barges were the firm's speciality and under his ownership the yard built the *Florence* (1877), *Muriel* (1880), *Eureka* (1880), *Una* (1882), *Glen Rosa* (1884), *Haste Away* (1886), and *Irex*, *Freston Tower* and *Dorothy* (1889). Cann also built the boomsail barges *Carisbrooke Castle*, 86 feet long, for Walker and Howard and the 88 foot *Mazeppa* for Harwich owners.

In 1889, at the height of all this activity, George Cann died from chest injuries sustained when crushed by a log being unloaded from a railway truck on

Harwich Quay. He was fifty-six years old and had four sons and two daughters. Two of the sons were destined to carry on the business. John Cann was a trained and dedicated shipwright already working in the yard. His brother Herbert had originally been a solicitor's clerk before joining the army. At the time of his father's death he was serving in Ireland. After a brief period of managership by the brother of George Cann, it was decided to continue the business as J. and H. Cann. John, who was an excellent craftsman but had limited business knowledge, acted as the practical partner and Herbert, who had been bought out of the army, returned to manage the financial affairs and curiously, to take charge of the small boat building shop, where up to three 14 foot boats could be built at once.

The barges and bawleys were built in the open and two sailing barges were building at the time of George Cann's death. The new firm continued this work as their main business, subsequently launching the spritties *May* (1891), *Mistley* (1891), *Susan* (1892), *Felix* (1893), *Ethel* (1894), *Centaur* (1895), *Kitty* (1895), *Bona* (1896), *Edme* (1898), *Marjorie* (1899), *Kimberley* (1900), *Gladys* (1901), *Resolute* (1903), *Memory* (1904), *Edith May* (1906) and *Leofleda* (1914). These barges were reputedly built from lines taken from skeleton half models made by John Cann and at least one of them was built with a few inches of rocker in the keel to anticipate and compensate for the inevitable hogging of the hull in trade.

A curious feature of the Cann yard was that the sailmaking firm of W. Pennick and Son was situated in the middle of its premises. They made the sails for many of the craft built by the Canns, including bawleys, and for other vessels. The yard sawpit was under the sail loft and there was also a blacksmith's shop where the ironwork was made. A set of barge blocks in the creek was close to the premises; barges were placed on these for repair to their flat bottoms, which could not be worked on in any other convenient way. Most of the English-grown timber used by the yard was purchased from Stour Wood at Wrabness or from Mann's timber yard at Earls Colne and was sawn from the tree in the yard. Originally this was done at the sawpit where the yard's sawyers Stephen Ainger and his son James worked full time for many years until powered saws were installed. The Aingers drove over in a trap each day from their home in Dovercourt, nearby.

About thirty men were employed at J. and H. Cann; a shipwright then earned between 25 and 28 shillings each week. In summer the yard bell rang to start at 6 am. All hands stopped for breakfast between 8 and 8.30 am. Work continued until 1 pm, with a dinner break until 2 pm, and ended at 5.30 pm. If the yard was busy the men had a tea break until 6 pm, then continued until 8 pm. This was a long and hard day's work. In winter the day started at 6.30 am and almost always stopped at 5.30 pm.

John Cann had tremendous enthusiasm for the work, retiring at 9 pm to rise at 5 am and be in good trim for the early start at the yard. At particularly

138

busy times he is said to have sometimes gone to bed with his boots still on, to save dressing time in the morning! John designed the craft built at the yard, first making skeleton half models. These were scaled from to produce offsets which it is thought were lofted full size before construction commenced. The spritsail barges were built in an average time of eight months and a bawley took five to six months to construct. Usually a new barge was laid down when one already building was planked and nearing completion. A new barge cost about £1000 in the period 1900–1914. One of the Cann family had a half-share in the barge *Ethel* and she went for her trial sail with the entire Cann family crowded on her deck for the day-long trip.

When John and Herbert Cann were newly established in business they built a barge whose owner complained that she leaked after a week or so in service. She was placed on the yard blocks for examination but no defects were found. Further complaints and repeated failure to find a leak made the Canns call the owner to their office and confront him with the challenge of taking either the barge or a cheque for her cost. The owner took the barge, as he knew these craft were usually built at a loss and when new could be re-sold for more than their original cost to the owner.

Cann's also built two small steamers for service on the rivers Orwell and Stour, named *Stour* and *Gipping* and about 70 feet long, besides doing considerable repair work to barges, bawleys and yachts and other craft. The boatbuilding shop reputedly turned out a 14 foot barge boat each week, most of them built on speculation and bought by barge owners locally and on the Thames and Medway. The Canns were also keen boat sailors and in 1908 they designed and started to build for themselves a 20 foot centreboard sloop for racing and day sailing. However, she was purchased while building by a yachtsman, who raced her successfully at Harwich, Aldeburgh and elsewhere.

Cann's built a number of bawleys including the *Maud* and the *Irene*, both built for members of the Good family, well known Harwich fishermen. Others were the *Olive Miriam, Gracie, Osprey, Doris, Unity, Onward, Two Brothers, Verona Iris, Helen and Violet* (or *Ellen and Violet*) and *Ellen*. These craft were usually planked in fir or Oregon pine, with garboards of English elm, on English oak sawn frames. John Cann's bawleys were shapely, with well formed transom, rounded forefoot and splendid hull sections. His work seems to have included the largest bawleys, about 42 feet long. Cann's built the 39 foot 6 inches bawley *Alice Matilda* as a speculation. She was sold in 1897 to the Young family of Leigh for £100, complete with all boat's gear.

The Leigh bawley *Olive Miriam* LO 3 was still working in 1938 though built in 1907. She was 35 feet 6 inches long with 13 foot 2 inches beam and drew 5 feet 6 inches. Her hull was typical of Cann's bawleys with a well formed entrance and the run ending in a shallow, almost delicately shaped transom. Cann's built the *Gracie* for J. or I. Emery of Leigh. She was very fast and won a challenge race at

139

Harwich against a Harwich bawley. Nowadays the best known of Cann's bawleys is the *Helen and Violet*, built in 1906 for James Kimber of Leigh and registered as LO 262. Unlike almost all the Colne and Blackwater smacks, several Leigh bawleys were worked for their owners, who in such instances were usually not fishermen but local shopkeepers and other small businessmen. The *Helen and Violet* was at first worked by Sidney Cotgrove, one of that redoubtable Leigh family of good fishermen. Two years later he handed over to Joseph Deal, of another line of Leigh stalwarts. In 1909 she was sold to Helen Irving of London, of whom nothing is known, but only a month later she reverted to Kimber's ownership and in September she was sold to Arthur Felton, a Leigh fishermen who was to sail her until 1927. The *Helen and Violet* is now owned at Brightlingsea and is used for pleasure sailing. She is 36 feet in length with 13 foot 9 inches beam and draws 4 feet 5 inches in her pleasure-sailing trim. The maximum sail area is 1655 square feet and individual areas are mainsail 1043 square feet, foresail 135 square feet, working jib 188 square feet, and jib-headed topsail 289 square feet.

In 1927 Arthur Felton sold the *Helen and Violet* to Christopher Cundey of Southend, who had a 15 hp engine installed. This was then a typical power unit for a craft of this size and use. Three years later she was sold to W. Annis of the well-known Brightlingsea fishing family, and in keeping with Colne usage she was converted to a boom and gaff mainsail. She was re-registered as CK 15 and was engaged in stowboating for sprats in winter and dredging for oysters on the Colne fishery at other times, when her crew were not away yachting. Unusually for the Colne, she was worked for Mr Annis by four local fishermen. The *Helen and Violet* survives as the fastest sailing bawley, though her old and speedier rival, the *Doris*, is also again in sailing trim and perhaps will once again assert herself in future racing.

The Canns may also have built the bawley *Band of Hope*, though this is not suggested by her shape. She fished until 1935, when she was sold to become a yacht. At 42 feet overall length she was one of the larger bawleys but her 13 foot beam and 5 foot draught are usual dimensions for shorter craft. Cann's yard flourished until it was closed about 1922, supposedly because of the difficulty of finding suitable timber, coupled with the advancing age of its owners. Another branch of the Cann family were painters, decorators and plumbers and did much work at the yards of Cann and also for Vaux.

The Norman family were other Harwich builders of bawleys. The original Norman, who is believed to have built several bawleys, was succeeded by his four sons Ike, Bill, Richard and Fred. They leased a piece of land at the end of West Street, Harwich, from the Great Eastern Railway Company and built at least two bawleys, one of them the *Wings of the Morning*. These were launched by being drawn on a wheeled cradle by horses to a nearby hard, to be floated off.

Vaux, another Harwich builder of small schooners and other merchant vessels and sailing barges, also built a few bawleys including the peculiarly named *Auto Da Fe* which won several bawley races at Harwich regatta before 1914. These were constructed at the old Harwich Navy Yard, which Vaux leased from the Admiralty. Considerable repair work was also carried out there. The bawleys were built under foreman James Garland, while the barge building and repair of light vessels was under foreman Christy. Vaux was followed at the Navy Yard by MacLearon, who was in turn followed by his son. Their occupation of the yard ended in 1930.

Races for bawleys were held as part of Harwich Town Regatta for many years before 1914, and the *Wings of the Morning* was a regular prizewinner.

As at Leigh, the Harwich fishermen quickly installed auxiliary engines and later had motor shrimping boats built. Sail died at Harwich before it was ousted at Leigh, and the number of craft fishing declined faster.

Fig. 103. John Cann, of the Harwich barge and bawley building family firm J. and H. Cann, proudly displays a half model, of one of his fast bawleys. This style of half model, in which the hull lines have been draughted before the model was made to prove them by eye, consisted of a

continued backboard on which the outline of the profile was drawn, then wooden sections were cut to the shape of the sections drawn on the plan and were erected on the board at the correct positions on the profile. The wooden stem, keel, deadwood and transom were added to scale, and longitudinal battens, representing ribbands, were bent around the sections and were fastened at stem and stern rebates. The resulting model gave an experienced eye a good idea of the hull's final form. The sections could be slightly altered if some imperfection was apparent. Similar models combined with draughting were used by many builders of small craft in north-east Essex. Aldous at Brightlingsea, where John Cann's father had been apprenticed, also used this method for many years and he probably copied it and passed it on to his son. By this method the Canns produced several notably fast bawleys and other small sailing craft.

Fig. 104. Rigged scale model of a Harwich bawley showing the single brail to the mainsail for shortening sail or temporarily furling. The stovepipe from the shrimp copper protrudes above the hatch covers and the bilge pump is rigged for display purposes on the port side amidships. The beam trawl for shrimping is on deck to starboard in this Science Museum photograph.

GLOSSARY

An explanation of some of the terms used in this book. The definitions are not exhaustive and have been restricted to clarification of terms in the sense and period covered by this history.

Barge .... In this book the term generally refers to the spritsail, cargo carrying barges of the east coast.

Belay .... To make a rope fast to a cleat, pin, bollard, cavil, etc. An order; "Belay the jib sheets".

Bermudian .... Bermudian rig. A main or mizzen sail, or the foresail of a schooner; of triangular shape set from the mast by slides running on a track, or by the luff rope fitting in a mast groove. Bermudian rig was revived for small racing yachts about 1911 and spread to the large racing yachts after 1919. The rig has since become predominant in sailing yachts, which were previously principally gaff rigged. Bermudian rig was commonly used by sailing craft in the West Indies at least 170 years ago. The rig as set by modern yachts is very efficient to windward and in large racers enabled the number of crew to be reduced.

Berth .... In shipbuilding a place on which a ship is built. "Building berth". A vessel is said to be "berthed" when she is moored alongside a quay or in a dock. i.e. "In her berth". To sailors, "getting a berth" meant obtaining a place in the crew of a vessel. In accommodation on board ship a berth meant a sleeping place for one man.

Board .... Making a tack to windward. "Making a board" (to windward). A term widely used but of obscure origin. The term may have been a survival from use of the "Traverse Board" for course plotting in seagoing ships.

Bobstay .... The chain or wire staying the end of the bowsprit to the stem.

Brig .... A small, square rigged cargo vessel or sailing warship. Brigs were much used on the east coast, particularly in the coal trade from the north-east coast to London.

Cable .... The anchor cable. Substantial chain or rope attached to an anchor and from which a vessel "rides" or lies at anchor.

Capstan .... A mechanical device for hauling ropes or tackles. A cylindrical barrel mounted on a spindle is turned by capstan bars thrust into slots in its top, which are pushed round by men. Alternatively, it may be turned by one or two handles, via gearing to the capstan barrel.

Cheesecutter .... A peaked, close fitting seafaring cap worn by captains, mates and others in yachts and smacks during the period covered by this book.

Clipper bow .... A form of stem which rises from the water in a graceful, forward curving line; in yachts usually ending with a small decorative emblem at deck level. The bowsprit protruded forward extending the outreach of this stem. The mid-19th century clipper ships generally had this type of bow.

Counter .... A counter stern. A usually graceful shape. In profile the under part of the vessel's stern rises at a gentle angle from the water and ends in a shapely and short, upward raking line. Counter sterns were used in most types of craft mentioned in this book.

Culch .... The clean shell, often oyster shell, laid broadcast over oyster layings before spring "spatfall"; the period of birth for young oysters which cling to the clean culch to commence their life cycle. Culch was often dredged from the sea bottom by sailing smacks who sold it to owners of layings.

Cutter .... A single masted sailing craft usually setting a gaff mainsail, staysail (or foresail), jib and a topsail set above the mainsail. A jib topsail is also often set above the jib. This is a most speedy, seaworthy rig and was usual for the Essex fishing smacks and for racing yachts. Yacht's cutter; the principal small sailing boat carried by a large yacht as one of her tenders.

Draughting .... Drawing. Usually refers to drawing plans. Draughtsman.

Dredging .... Oyster dredging. A form of fishing by smacks towing oyster dredges along the sea bottom by dredge warps to gather oysters.

Fetch .... To sail towards and arrive at a certain position despite the wind and weather. e.g. "to fetch a mark", "to fetch a port".

Fish .... To catch fish. Quantity of fish. Alternatively, to repair a broken spar or mast by supporting it with spare spars or other improvised items such as hand-spikes, etc., which are bound to it with rope, like splints.

Fo'csle, or forecastle .... The forward compartment of a sailing vessel's hull. In yachts, small smacks and traditional merchant ships this was the space where the crew lived. In large smacks the crew usually lived aft and the fo'csle was used as a store.

Foresail .... More fully: "Forestaysail". An alternative term commonly used for the "staysail" in sailing vessels, (see staysail). In a schooner the large fore and aft sail set on the foremast is termed the foresail.

Gaff .... The spar supporting the head of a gaff sail. Hoisted and lowered by the throat and peak halyards.

Gig .... A long, clencher built rowing boat pulled by four to eight men and usually between 22 - 32 feet in length. Carried by large yachts for the owner's use before small steam and later motor launches became common.

Gun punt .... A small, low, pointed stern boat used by wildfowlers and generally mounting a long barrelled, fixed gun.

Headsails .... Staysails, jibs and jib-topsails are frequently referred to as "Headsails". i.e. sails at the "head" or forward end of a vessel.

Jackyard topsail .... A large topsail in gaff rigged craft, principally used by racing yachts. The luff (forward end) was extended above the masthead by the topsail yard and the clew (after, upper corner) was extended beyond the end of the gaff by a "jackyard". Jackyard topsails were also sometimes set in light weather by working craft.

Jib topsail .... A triangular sail set from the topmast head, down the fore topmast stay above the jib. Racing yachts usually set three types of jib topsail; the "Long roper" (large), the "Baby" (small) and the "Yankee".

Ketch .... A two masted sailing vessel with gaff or bermudian sails on each mast. The after or mizzen mast is shorter than the mainmast (the forward mast) and is stepped forward of the vessel's stern-post or rudder stock.

Lift .... More correctly "Topping lift". The item of running rigging used to raise or "top" (lift) a boom. In small craft a single rope. In smacks and yachts usually also fitted with a purchase to give adequate power.

Luff .... The forward edge of a sail. In a gaff or bermudian sail the edge abaft the mast. To luff; the act of steering a craft closer or into the wind.

Mastheadsman .... A sailor with special duties aloft, particularly in a racing yacht. Large yachts had a first and second mastheadsman; positions of extra pay and advancement.

Mingle .... A wooden or iron instrument used to discharge sprats from a stowboat net. Mingles were placed under the after end of a net and parted off the desired amount of its contents for discharge on deck or down the fish hatch. This quantity was termed a 'cod' (about four bushels).

Mizzen .... The after mast or sail set on the after mast, in a ketch or yawl rigged vessel. The after mast of a square rigged vessel, other than a brig or brigantine.

"One-design" .... When all the craft of a racing class are built and equipped exactly alike to ensure that skill in handling decides the result of a race they are termed "One-design". Originally more fully; "One class—one design".

Oyster Dredge .... A triangular shaped iron frame with a cross bar and hoeing edge, having a rectangular shaped net with an iron mesh bottom and fibre net upper part or back, and tapering sides. The net is held parallel to the hoeing edge at its rear end by a cross stick laced to it. Dredges were generally of two sizes; small ones about three feet across the hoe and large or deep sea dredges often six feet or rather more, across the hoe or "scythe". Dredges were towed by bass rope warps from the smack, in varying numbers depending on the work.

Oyster dredgers .... Fishermen cultivating or gathering oysters with dredges towed by smacks or oyster skiffs. Alternatively, smacks engaged in an oyster fishery.

Oyster layings .... Areas of a river or creek noted for the good growth of oysters. Usually clearly marked by withies (saplings driven into the bottom with their heads above water). Layings were frequently owned by individuals; oyster dredgers and merchants.

Oyster skiff .... A beamy, shallow draught, clench-built open boat about 18 - 25 feet in length, used for transporting oysters from smacks to shore, or to oyster layings. Usually rowed or sculled by an oar over the stern.

Plater .... A tradesman skilled in iron or steel shipbuilding. Platers commonly style themselves "Boilermakers" after the origins of their trade.

Prize money .... Paid to crews of racing yachts, or smacks racing in regattas, from the money given as a prize. In racing yachts prize money formed a substantial supplement to the crew's wages, which for a hand in a fast yacht might be almost be doubled thereby. Racing yachts' captains and mates received a larger proportion of the prize money than the hands.

Quarter .... The sides of a vessel's stern. i.e. the port and starboard quarters.

Raking .... Rake. As applied to a vessel's rig this means at an angle to the vertical. e.g. "raking masts"; masts sloping aft. "Rakish"; with much rake or speedy looking.

Ratlines .... Ropes secured at vertical intervals between the shrouds supporting a mast to provide a "ladder" for climbing the shrouds to the mast heads.

Reef .... To reduce the area of a sail by reefing. The position line of a reef across a sail. To reef; act of reefing. Reefed. Reef points; short lengths of rope sewn to a sail at the line of a reef. The sail below the reef points is bunched up after the reef pendants have been hauled taut (see reef pendants) and the points tied under the sail in a knot, reducing the sail area.

Reef pendants .... Stout ropes which are rove through "cringles" (reinforced holes) at the luff and leech (forward and after edges) of a sail and which are hauled down taut to the boom before tying the reef points. e.g. "Hauling down a reef". "Shake out a reef"; to untie the reef points and release the pendants to restore sail area.

Rigger .... A skilled man usually employed by a shipyard or yachtyard to make and overhaul rigging. Often an ex-seaman with exceptional skill in working with fibre or steel rope.

Ruck, rucked .... When the peak or upper end of a gaff sail is lowered by its halyard to swing freely, while the luff remained set up taut, the peak is said to be "rucked", rendering the sail less powerful in driving effect. A manoeuvre much used to regulate a vessel's speed when fishing, coming to anchor or moorings, or to ease her in bad weather. An alternative term for ruck is to "scandalise" a gaff sail.

"Runners" or running backstays .... Stays supporting a mast at the "hounds" and leading aft. These were usually of wire (the runner pendant), the windward of which was set up by a tackle (the runner tackle).

Salvager .... A seaman or a smack engaged in giving assistance to a stranded or wrecked vessel, particularly in winter: helping to save life or remove cargo and equipment from wrecks.

Schooner .... A two or more masted sailing vessel with the masts of equal, or almost equal, height and fore and aft sails, either gaff or bermudian, set on each mast, also having headsails forward of the foremast. Schooners fitted with square topsails were termed "topsail schooners".

Scope .... The amount of cable let out and to which a vessel lays at anchor. e.g. "Give her more scope; pay out more cable.

Set .... A fore and aft sail is set when it is hoisted. A square sail may be set when it is loosed from the yard and sheeted.

Sheer .... The line of a vessel's profile at deck or the top of the bulwarks; usually a gentle curve. "A sweeping sheer". Alternatively, sheer; to move obliquely through the water, commonly against the tide: "to take a sheer".

"Shifters" or shifting backstays. .... Stays supporting a topmast head and leading aft. These were usually of wire (the shifter pendant) which was set up by a tackle (the shifter tackle). They were called "Shifters" because, unlike the runners, they had to be "shifted" i.e. slacked right off and the windward one set up, at each tack the vessel made.

Shrouds .... Wire rope rigging transversely supporting a mast and set taut with rigging screws or "deadeyes and lanyards". Before c. 1870 shrouds were usually of hemp rope, which stretched badly.

Smack .. A cutter or ketch rigged sailing vessel used for fishing. These craft were developed to near perfection by the Essex fishermen and shipbuilders.

Spit .... The point of a shoal.

Spitfire .... A small storm jib.

Spreaders .... A pair of struts supporting topmast shrouds on a mast. An earlier term was "Crosstrees".

Staysail .... The triangular sail immediately forward of the mainmast or foremast in fore and aft rigged craft. More fully, forestaysail (see foresail).

Stem .... The forward member or edge of a vessel's bow.

Stowboat net. (Stow net) .... The large, close-meshed, funnel-shaped sprat net of the Essex and Hampshire fisheries. It is now obsolete. Dating from the Middle Ages this was earlier known as the "stall net" from the smack setting it lying at anchor with the net beneath her, when fishing.

Topmast .... An addition to the head of the lowermast usually attached to its forward side and arranged to "house" or lower when required either for relieving strain on the vessel in bad weather or for repair. Most of the Essex smacks and the gaff rigged yachts were fitted with topmasts which could be housed.

Topsail .... The sail set from a topmast above a gaff main or mizzen sail, or above the gaff foresail in a schooner. Also a "square topsail" in square rigged vessels such as brigs, barques, etc., or in a topsail schooner.

Trawl .... A fishing net and associated gear for catching bottom-swimming fish and shrimps. The "beam trawl" was the type used by the sailing smacks. A triangular shaped net spread behind a wooden beam which might be 25 - 35 feet long. This was towed astern of the smack, along the sea bottom, by a rope warp which passed through a large block attached to the trawl heads at each end of the beam by a rope bridle. The net was attached at the upper forward edge to the beam by lacings, and at the bottom forward edge to a ground rope between the heads, which might be weighted to seek out fish lying close to the bottom. At each end of the beam an iron trawl head carried it above the bottom in a sledge-like manner. The trawl nets mesh varied with the type of fish to be caught. The smallest mesh being used for shrimps. When trawling, fish entered the net's mouth and were trapped in its apex called the "cod end". Those attempting to escape back towards the mouth along the net were caught in pockets in the wings or sides. The trawl was hauled up by the trawl warp by hand, or with the aid of a hand capstan in the Essex smacks.

Trim .... The adjustment of a vessel's floating disposition longitudinally or transversely. e.g. "Trimmed by the stern"; a vessel drawing more water aft than forward. To trim sheets (of sails); to adjust the sheets. To trim cargo; to level or adjust it for the best seaworthiness.

Truss, trice-up .... When the tack of a gaff sail is lifted part way up the mast by a tricing line (truss) or tackle, the tack is said to be "triced up".

Trysail .... A sail of moderate area usually set as a substitute for the mainsail in storms, or in case of accident to the mainsail. Large racing yachts set a trysail for passagemaking to preserve the set of the racing mainsail. A storm trysail was of much smaller area than a mainsail and was made of stouter sailcloth. Until about 1914 trysails were usually quadrilateral and were set by a trysail gaff. In later years they were increasingly triangular.

Ways .... Long wooden timbers of rectangular section placed under a vessel to be launched. There were two sets; the fixed or "ground ways" and the upper or "sliding ways". The surface between them was well greased to permit easy movement when the time came for the launch. Similar ways were sometimes used in small yards to haul vessels out of the water. They were also commonly used to "strike over" craft of all sizes and types which needed to be moved about in a ship or yacht yard.

Windlass .... The mechanism for raising an anchor. The Essex smacks were fitted with a primitive wooden windlass, the barrel of which was rotated by two handspikes fitting into slots and turned by one or more men. Several turns of the chain cable were taken round the barrel which could be retained by a ratchet pawl. After about 1850 most yachts had a compact iron windlass of patent design, or an iron capstan.

Yawl .... A two masted sailing vessel with gaff or bermudian sails on each mast. The after or mizzen mast is considerably shorter than the mainmast and is stepped aft of the sternpost or rudder stock.

INDEX

148

Other titles by John Leather
published by Terence Dalton Limited

THE NORTHSEAMEN

A story of the fishermen, yachtsmen and shipbuilders
of the Colne and Blackwater

THE SALTY SHORE

A story of the smugglers, wildfowlers, fishermen
and bargemen of the Blackwater